Better Homes and Gardens.

MAINTAINING YOUR HOME

BETTER HOMES AND GARDENS® BOOKS

Editor: Gerald M. Knox
Art Director: Ernest Shelton
Managing Editor: David A. Kirchner
Copy and Production Editors: James D. Blume, Marsha Jahns,
Mary Helen Schiltz, Carl Voss

Associate Art Directors: Linda Ford Vermie, Neoma Alt West,
Randall Yontz
Assistant Art Directors: Lynda Haupert, Harijs Priekulis,
Tom Wegner
Senior Graphic Designers: Mike Eagleton, Lyne Neymeyer,
Stan Sams
Graphic Designers: Mike Burns, Sally Cooper, Jack Murphy,
Darla Whipple-Frain, Brian Wignall, Kim Zarley

Vice President, Editorial Director: Doris Eby
Group Editorial Services Director: Duane L. Gregg

Senior Vice President, General Manager: Fred Stines
Director of Publishing: Robert B. Nelson
Vice President, Retail Marketing: Jamie Martin
Vice President, Direct Marketing: Arthur Heydendael

All About Your House: Maintaining Your Home

Project Editor: James A. Hufnagel
Associate Editors: Willa Rosenblatt Speiser, Leonore A. Levy
Copy and Production Editor: Marsha Jahns
Building and Remodeling Editor: Joan McCloskey
Furnishings and Design Editor: Shirley Van Zante
Garden Editor: Douglas A. Jimerson
Money Management and Features Editor: Margaret Daly

Associate Art Director: Randall Yontz
Graphic Designer: Harijs Priekulis
Electronic Text Processor: Donna Russell

Contributing Editors: Stephen Mead and Jill Abeloe Mead
Contributors: Mary Bryson, John H. Ingersoll, Paul Kitzke,
Leonore A. Levy, Willa Rosenblatt Speiser, Marcia Spires,
and Michael D. Walsh

Special thanks to Stephen and Elinor Chase, Bill Hopkins, Jr.,
Babs Klein, Scott Little, and Don Wipperman for their valuable
contributions to this book.

INTRODUCTION

Stocks, bonds, and other financial instruments are important ways to achieve monetary security, but for a great many families, a home is by far their most significant asset—an investment that almost always grows in value over the years. In at least two respects, however, a home differs significantly from other types of investments. One is that you can live in it; another is that a home, unlike stock certificates, must be conscientiously maintained if you're to realize its full potential.

Well-maintained homes appreciate more rapidly than houses that are neglected. They're more enjoyable to live in, too. But the biggest reason for keeping a home at its best, we believe, has to do with something called pride of ownership.

Maintaining Your Home is about pride of ownership—the subtle satisfactions that tell the world (and yourselves) that your home is important to the people who live there.

You may or may not find pleasure in mowing a lawn, cleaning out gutters, fighting the grime that besieges interior surfaces, tidying up kitchens and baths, changing furnace filters, or the dozens of other jobs that constitute good home maintenance. All of these, however, are tasks that get easier once you know exactly what to do, and then do them a few times.

Maintaining Your Home begins with your home's yard and exterior, then moves inside to tell about taking care of interior surfaces, the kitchen and baths, major appliances, furnishings, and systems. Lastly, the book turns to ways you can reduce maintenance at your house, and offers guidance about how to go about replacing materials and equipment when they finally wear out.

We hope that *Maintaining Your Home* will help make yours a house you can truly be proud of. We hope, too, that you'll take a look at other volumes in the Better Homes and Gardens® ALL ABOUT YOUR HOUSE Library. This comprehensive series of books explores just about every aspect of improving, furnishing, managing, and maintaining a modern-day home.

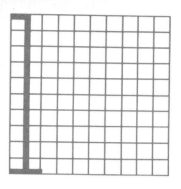

SURVEYING YOUR HOME'S MAINTENANCE NEEDS

Good maintenance is mainly a matter of habit: You first determine what regular chores need to be done around your home—and when—then set agendas to help you carry them out. This introductory chapter looks at the major maintenance categories around most homes, then directs you to subsequent chapters that explore each in greater detail.

In some respects, *Maintaining Your Home* is the story of a single house—the one pictured *opposite*.

The house, as you can see, is a two-story, clapboard-sided Colonial, constructed either immediately before or just after World War II. At the time we found it, the house had been languishing, unoccupied for nearly six months, in a sluggish real estate market. We rented the home for use as a combination photo studio and test lab where we could develop the information for this book.

We chose this particular house because it had maintenance problems common to most homes. Though far from falling apart, it had been neglected—especially during those months of emptiness. By identifying and solving the maintenance problems at *our* house, we hope to help you identify and solve the maintenance problems at *your* house.

For example, at the time we took possession of the house, its landscaping differed dramatically from the trim, tidy yard shown here. As at many older homes, trees and shrubs were overgrown, crowding pathways, trapping moisture against siding, even rubbing away roofing. The steeply sloped lawn was bald and eroding in some spots, weedy in others. A retaining wall was beginning to collapse, and an ill-placed tree was obscuring one of the home's most attractive features—its pedimented front entry. Our first task, we decided, was to prune, plant, and get this yard back into a condition that could be maintained easily. Chapter 2—"Your Yard"—documents what we did here, explains how to spot and eliminate maintenance problems your yard might have, and gives guidance on setting up your own particular yard maintenance agenda.

Take a walk
As you stroll around your property and note landscaping features you'd like to change, be honest with yourself. It's all well and good to resolve that you'll take on one heavy job this year, another the next, but you might be better off to hire a landscape contractor to put things right once and for all. That's what we did, and the entire project took only a day and a half.

Level with yourself, also, about just how much yard maintenance you're willing to do. No landscaping can totally take care of itself, but in Chapter 9—"Minimizing Maintenance"—you can learn about ways to cut down on the amount of time you spend mowing, weeding, pruning, and raking.

Finally, invest in the right tools to get the job done. High-quality hand tools, kept sharp and clean, greatly reduce the amount of effort you have to expend, and do better work, too. Power equipment, such as mowers, cultivators, weeders, snowblowers, hedge clippers, and the like, also can be big time- and labor-savers, but avoid the temptation to overinvest in equipment that can itself become a maintenance headache.

SURVEYING YOUR HOME'S MAINTENANCE NEEDS

THE EXTERIOR

A well-groomed house makes a favorable impression on visitors and neighbors, but maintaining your home's exterior is more than just a matter of keeping up appearances. Weather is the big enemy out here: On clear days, sunlight heats up exterior materials and causes them to expand; in cool weather, those same surfaces contract. With almost continual expanding and contracting, small cracks are bound to show up somewhere—and small cracks soon turn into big ones that can damage your home's structure and interior.

Like its landscaping, the exterior of our home had some problems. Its roofing, flashings, gutters, and downspouts were nearly worn out and would soon need replacing.

The siding was in better condition, with a fairly recent coat of paint, but some boards were splitting and the paint was blistering and scaling in some areas, as you can see in the photograph *at left*. Caulking around windows and other exterior elements was beginning to fail, too, opening pathways to moisture that can ruin insulation and even structural members.

All this seemed discouraging at first, until we realized that we could solve most of these problems, and even prolong the roof's life for a few years, with less than $100 worth of materials.

The main expenditures were for a few tubes of caulking, a can of roofing cement, sheet metal flashing material, paint, and a couple of pieces of wood siding. Tools also were inexpensive—step and extension ladders, a couple of paint scrapers, a caulking gun, a putty knife, and several paintbrushes.

Chapter 3—"Your Home's Exterior"—shows how we set about solving these problems, then goes on to tell how to give your home a top-to-bottom checkup, identify its exterior maintenance needs, and set up your own outside maintenance agenda.

Points to ponder

As you analyze your home's exterior surfaces and their upkeep needs, keep these general points in mind.
• Older materials, like older cars, demand more maintenance than newer ones. Roofing is a good example. With a new roof you need only check every so often for lifted shingles, downed tree limbs, and other possible damage. As the roof ages, its flashings begin to deteriorate, shingles dry out and crack, and gutters sag and rust through. After patching, repatching, and hoping for the best, you'll eventually need to shop for a new roof.

When materials fail, be prepared with information about new ones that will reduce your maintenance load. Pages 136 and 137 in Chapter 9 detail your exterior materials options.
• Make safety a prime maintenance consideration. Attend to loose railings immediately, before someone takes a bad spill. The same goes for cracked steps, broken windows, and ice-clogged gutters. Chimneys pose a twofold safety hazard: Loose masonry could fall and injure someone, and a sooty chimney could catch fire. To learn about maintaining chimneys, see page 49.
• Finally, realize that anything you do to keep weather *out* also helps keep expensive heating and cooling energy *in*. Cracks in siding, at the foundation, and at hose bibs, and other items that penetrate your home's skin, can add surprising amounts to your utility bills. Make sure, too, that all windows and doors are tightly weather-stripped. Pages 44 and 45 tell about your weather-stripping choices.

SURVEYING YOUR HOME'S MAINTENANCE NEEDS

THE INSIDE

You probably see a lot more of the inside of your home than you do its exterior. Here the big enemies are dirt and everyday wear and tear. Flooring materials require almost daily care to keep looking their best. Walls grow dusty and dingy over time. Hardware grows contrary with age. Few people truly enjoy housecleaning, but with the right equipment and routines, you can keep dirt at bay.

Perhaps one day soon someone will invent a self-cleaning house. You would simply set a dial, walk out the door, and return an hour or so later to a home that's sparkling clean. Until then, however, homeowners will have to continue dealing with dirt the old-fashioned way—with vacuums, buckets, mops, brooms, and elbow grease.

Compared to the yard and exterior, the interior of our house was in good condition. Walls and woodwork had been painted recently. Oak flooring, protected for years by carpeting, needed only a good buffing. Most doors and windows operated smoothly.

We did find a few minor difficulties, such as sticking windows, squeaking hinges, and balky latches. These were easily set right, as you'll learn in Chapter 4—''Inside Your Home.''

The big discovery we made in producing Chapter 4 is that high-quality tools make housecleaning jobs much easier. People typically assemble their cleaning-tool kits an item or two at a time, often from the limited selections on grocery store shelves. In shopping for the cleaning implements you'll see in Chapter 4, we decided to try a different tactic and visited a firm that specializes in selling janitorial supplies.

We found that tools designed to be used day in, day out by custodial crews are much more durable than flimsy home versions. They're easier to use, too, and do a better job in less time.

If you'd like to clean your house more efficiently, review the contents of your cleaning closet, make a list of items you'd like to upgrade, and take a trip to a janitorial supplies dealer. You probably won't have to return for years.

Getting help
Gone are the days, for most households, of live-in maids who attended to every cleaning chore. Now homeowners either handle housecleaning themselves, often on a catch-as-catch-can basis, or hire professional help to come in by the day or chore.

If you find yourself putting off cleaning jobs until things are really bad, consider investing—at least periodically—in the services of a cleaning professional. The box on page 107 explains what they have to offer.

Another way to help reduce cleaning chores, no matter who does them, is to invest in easy-maintenance interior surface materials. No-wax flooring, wipe-clean wall coverings, mar-resistant polyurethane finishes, and dozens of other products have all but eliminated entire categories of drudgery. Pages 138 and 139 tell about these.

Wall and floor surfaces make up a big part of a home's interior, but they're far from all of it. Kitchens and baths, appliances, furniture, and heating and cooling systems all have their own special maintenance needs. More about these on the pages (and in the chapters) that follow.

THE
KITCHEN
AND BATHS

Kitchens and baths have unique maintenance problems. Because they're mess zones, they have to stand up to repeated scrubbings, spills and splashes, heavy doses of humidity, and—in the case of kitchens—heat and grease. What's more, kitchens and baths are where most of a home's plumbing fixtures are located, and plumbing requires its own special maintenance procedures.

Analyze which rooms in your home are the busiest, and you'll probably conclude that the kitchen and bath (or baths) win hands down. Maintaining these high-activity zones is an ongoing process made no easier by the fact that you must contend with a diverse collection of components.

Because kitchens and baths are so busy and complex, we've devoted an entire chapter—and more—to telling how to maintain them. Here's a survey of what you'll find in Chapter 5 and later.
• Plumbing, the core of every kitchen and bath, demands next to no attention until something goes wrong. When a

drain backs up, however, or a faucet begins dripping, you have to take action. Pages 84–87 tell how to keep plumbing operable.
• Cabinet doors and drawers don't require regular maintenance either, but one that doesn't open or close smoothly is a constant annoyance. If you have balky cabinet hardware in your kitchen or bath, consult pages 82 and 83.
• Wood, vinyl, stainless steel, ceramic tile, aluminum, porcelain—kitchens and baths typically abound in a variety of surface materials that must be cleaned, or at least wiped off, on a daily basis. Knowing

exactly which cleaning product to use on each not only makes cleaning easier, it also can prolong the materials' life spans and keep them looking their best. A chart on page 89 compares kitchen and bath cleaning products and tells which application each works best for.

One important set of kitchen components you *won't* find discussed in Chapter 5 is appliances. These are stars of their own chapter. More about them on the following pages.

Finally, if you're thinking about remodeling your kitchen or replacing it with a brand-new one, pages 140 and 141 tell how to make minimal maintenance part of the plan.

MAJOR APPLIANCES

The machines that cool our food, cook it, clean dishes, and wash and dry clothes are easy to take for granted. After all, aren't major appliances specifically designed to deliver years of maintenance-free service? Well, almost. It's true that most refrigerators no longer need defrosting and many ovens clean themselves, but periodically attending to appliances saves you money in two ways: The equipment lasts longer, and it operates more efficiently, which conserves energy.

If you've ever had to call for service when a major appliance conks out, you already know that appliance repairs aren't cheap. Often you have to pay not only for the parts and labor required but also for related expenses and inconveniences such as spoiled food, restaurant meals, or laundry costs.

Just a little preventive maintenance can reduce the number of service calls you have to make, and perhaps help you anticipate others. Chapter 6—"Major Appliances"—treats individual appliances in detail. Here are some general points that apply to all appliances.

• Keep them clean. Dust, grease, food spills, and lint can gradually choke an appliance. Most people diligently keep the visible parts of appliances clean, but what about the places you can't see, such as refrigerator coils or the dryer exhaust system? Dust and lint cause motors to run hotter than they should, which greatly shortens their lives. Pages 94–99 tell how to clean appliances' vital working parts.

• Keep them level. All major appliances come with leveling devices, usually adjustable feet you turn to compensate for any irregularities in the floor. These were probably adjusted when the appliance was installed, but vibration can loosen them. Check each unit periodically with a level. Some motor-driven appliances, such as washing machines, can beat themselves to an early death if they're not level. Page 97 shows how to level major appliances.

• Check gaskets. All major appliances have door gaskets—to keep heat in an oven, for example, or out of a refrigerator. A gasket that's not doing its job properly impairs the appliance's efficiency, costing you money and maybe putting additional strain on the machine. Pages 97–99 also explain how to check and replace gaskets.

• Be alert for signs—and sounds—of trouble. Often, appliances broadcast early warnings that they're not working properly. A refrigerator motor that cycles on and off more often than usual, for example, may be telling you that the thermostat or defrost timer is malfunctioning—and either condition could soon burn out the motor and compressor. Pages 100 and 101 present an appliance-by-appliance troubleshooting checklist that can help you detect and solve small problems before they turn into big ones.

Shopping for new appliances

Eventually, despite your best maintenance efforts, appliances just wear out and need replacing. When that happens, refer to pages 146 and 147 in Chapter 10 for basics about appliance buymanship, and to pages 150 and 151 for information about conserving energy with new appliances and other household equipment.

FURNISHINGS

In a sense, furnishings are your home's clothing—and like clothes, furnishings need to be clean to look their best. That's more easily said than done, however, when you consider all the different fabrics, woods, metals, and other materials that help furnish a modern home. How can you keep up with all of them without spending nearly all your time at it?

One thing that makes furnishings different from other elements of your home is that they're movable. You can rearrange them whenever you like, take them along if you move, and hand cherished pieces down for several generations. Clearly, it pays to properly maintain these important family assets.

As with maintaining just about anything, taking care of furnishings demands that you overcome the natural tendency to put things off. Neglect a spill and it will soon set into a stain that could be difficult or even impossible to remove. Put off deep-cleaning fabrics and dust will eventually begin to wear away their fibers.

Taking immediate and timely action isn't difficult once you know which cleaning products and processes work best in a particular situation. Most fresh stains, for example, fade away fast when they're treated with the proper remedy. Charts on pages 112 and 113 in Chapter 7 give first aid treatments for stains in fabric and wood furnishings.

Dust, a ubiquitous abrasive that scratches wood finishes and chews away at fibers, may be the biggest single destroyer of furnishings. Regular cleaning and periodic deep-cleaning neutralize dust's destruction. Pages 106–109 tell how to keep dust at bay with fabric, leather, and vinyl upholstery; pages 110 and 111 tell about maintaining wood furniture.

Preventive maintenance applies to furnishings, too. You may not be able to spare a sofa from the occasional spilled ice cream cone or soft drink, but you can—and should—shield it from perils such as condensation, excess humidity, and the sun's bleaching rays. Pages 106–111 present preventive maintenance measures for all sorts of furnishings.

Revive tired furnishings— or replace them?
Loose joints, minor tears, sagging springs, and other signs of age or heavy use eventually afflict most furnishings. Often all that's needed is a minor repair, but in some cases you might have to face up to a major refinishing or reupholstering project. Chapter 7 can help you decide whether to save a piece of furniture or discard it.

When you are in the market for new furnishings, keep maintenance considerations in mind as you shop. Oiled wood, for example, has a rich, natural sheen, but many oiled pieces have to be reoiled every month or so. Choose an oiled finish for a heavily used dining table and you could be setting yourself up for a maintenance headache.

In general, better-quality furniture is easier to maintain and lasts longer, but keep in mind that some furniture categories have predictable life spans. For example, upholstered pieces in everyday use typically must be reupholstered or replaced after 10 to 15 years, no matter how well you maintain them. On the other hand, case goods—cabinets, chests, desks, wall units, headboards, and tables—can last almost indefinitely. This means that if you're in the beginning stages of furnishing a home or apartment, you might choose to skimp a bit on the quality level of upholstered pieces and invest the savings in case goods that will be with you for years to come, long after you've upgraded the upholstered furniture.

SYSTEMS

Heating, cooling, plumbing, and wiring—a home's largely unseen lifelines—are easily ignored until something goes wrong. When a furnace breaks down, however, or a pipe freezes, you face what amounts to a household catastrophe. Fortunately, with just a few ounces of preventive maintenance, you can avert most systems disasters.

Compared to the rigors of yard work or the day-in, day-out duties of housecleaning, maintaining your home's systems is easy. You need only tend to them from time to time, keep watch to be sure everything is running smoothly, and be prepared to take prompt action when something breaks down.

If you're intimidated by the thought of dealing with the mechanical intricacies of heating, cooling, plumbing, and wiring, Chapter 8 can allay your fears. It introduces you to each of your home's systems, explains how they work, details specific maintenance needs, and presents troubleshooting checklists to help you diagnose—and often solve—systems problems. Here's a system-by-system preview of what you'll find in Chapter 8 and elsewhere in the book.

Heating and cooling
Keeping heating and cooling systems running smoothly mainly calls for simple, screwdriver-and-pliers tasks once or twice a year. You need to change filters, keep compressor units breathing freely, make minor adjustments, and periodically have the system checked out by a heating contractor. Pages 118–125 tell what you need to know, whether your home is heated with gas, oil, or electricity, forced air, hot water, or steam.

Eventually, even well-maintained heating and cooling equipment reaches the end of its allotted life span, and when that happens, you're faced with finding a replacement, often in a hurry. Chapter 10—"When Things Just Wear Out"—steers you through the process of selecting new units, tells how to evaluate energy

cost considerations, and explains what you need to know about warranties and service.

Plumbing
Most plumbing problems happen at fixtures. Drains clog, faucets drip, and toilets gurgle and waste water. Because plumbing fixtures are mostly located in kitchens and baths, we've included solutions to fixture problems in Chapter 5, pages 84–87.

Occasionally, however, plumbing difficulties occur farther down the line. Pipes sweat and sometimes spring minor leaks. Worse yet, they can freeze and do major damage if you don't thaw them immediately. Pages 126–131 in Chapter 8 tell how to deal with—and prevent—pipe-related maladies.

Electricity
Of all a home's major systems, wiring requires the least maintenance and has the fewest problems. That's probably fortunate, because for many people electricity is also the most mysterious force in their homes.

Actually, as you'll discover in Chapter 8, electricity behaves in very clear-cut, easy to understand ways. Learn about them and you can diagnose and solve many electrical problems yourself. The chapter also tells how to determine whether your home has adequate power for today's needs and how to keep track of energy consumption by reading your own meter.

THE LOW-MAINTENANCE HOUSE

Like the self-cleaning house, the zero-maintenance house is an idea whose time has not yet arrived. There are ways, however, to greatly reduce the amounts of time, energy, and money you spend on maintenance chores. Here's a survey of strategies for cutting down the upkeep requirements at your house.

What's the maintenance chore that you like least? Perhaps you're sick of the endless rounds of scraping, patching, caulking, and painting that wood siding demands. Or maybe you begrudge the evening and weekend hours devoted to yard work. Whatever your pet maintenance peeve, consider budgeting funds to reduce the hassle or eliminate it entirely.

Inside, outside, and all around your home, money invested in minimizing maintenance pays dividends for as long as you own the house, and also can add to its value.

To understand the benefits of investing in low maintenance, consider this hypothetical example: Your kitchen is serviceable but out of date. Just cleaning up after dinner takes 30 minutes or more, thanks to worn surfaces, old appliances that collect dirt and grease, and cabinet space so tight you have to perform juggling feats every time you put away the plates or cookware.

An all-new kitchen—cabinets, counters, flooring, appliances, the works—might cost $8,000, for example. It's not unrealistic to expect that a new kitchen, especially one planned for easy cleanability, could cut in half the time you spend maintaining it. That's more than an hour and a half a week, just for dinner cleanup alone, plus at least another hour and a half for tidying up after other meals and maintenance routines such as scrubbing the floor and cleaning the oven.

It's hard to put a dollar value on leisure time, but three hours a week adds up to more than six days a year you could devote to something more rewarding than scullery work. What's more, should you decide to sell your home, the new kitchen could add as much as 10 percent to your home's value.

Planning low-maintenance improvements

Chapter 9—"Minimizing Maintenance"—surveys the major maintenance areas we've covered on the preceding pages and tells about improvements that can lighten the work load—and usually make your home more enjoyable, as well. Most are not nearly as expensive as a new kitchen, and some—such as reorganizing storage—cost next to nothing. Here are some other strategies that can help make yours a low-maintenance house.

• Make minimizing maintenance an important consideration in any major project you're contemplating. If you're planning to add on, for example, you might come out dollars ahead in the long run to re-side the entire house at the same time. The new exterior will be easier to take care of, and the addition will blend in perfectly.

• Set up a program you can accomplish in stages. Landscaping, especially, lends itself to staged development. This year you might revamp and replant the front yard. Next year, the time you save caring for it might be devoted to improving the side and back yards.

• Be realistic about what you can and can't do yourself. Many low-maintenance materials, such as new vinyl soffits like the one shown *at left*, are packaged by home centers with amateurs in mind. On the other hand, a bigger project, especially one such as installing a new kitchen, is best left to professionals, who can get the job done with a minimum of disruption to everyday life.

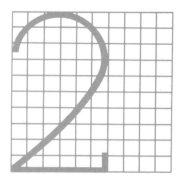

2

YOUR
YARD

For better or worse, your yard provides the setting for your home. One can't look its best if the other isn't up to comparable standards. Taking care of a yard isn't complicated or mysterious. Luck, a green thumb, and extensive equipment may help, but organization is the key. Mostly, yard maintenance means keeping track of what needs to be done, then setting priorities and carrying out the tasks on your list at the right times. This chapter shows how we brought the All About Your House yard back into shape after a period of relatively lax maintenance, and then tells how to establish a maintenance agenda for your own yard.

IDENTIFYING LANDSCAPING PROBLEMS

Outdoor maintenance and gardening chores are, to some extent, what you make them. Nevertheless, certain basic problems typically crop up, and the solutions to them vary according to your situation.

• If you're moving into a newly built home, landscape planning and nurturing are probably your foremost tasks. Problems are likely to include coddling a newly seeded lawn or coaxing fledgling shrubs through difficult winters, long dry spells, or other environmental crises.

• If you've recently purchased an older home, you're taking on someone else's yard maintenance standards. Shrubs may be trimmed to perfection, and the lawn may be green from March to December thanks to weekly deep watering. Or, flower beds may be overgrown and trees in dire need of trimming. It's up to you to live up to—or down to—those standards. For more about deciding just how much maintenance is right for you, see pages 36 and 37.

• If you've lived in one place for several years, you may find that your yard's maintenance needs have changed, or that your interest in maintaining your yard is greater or less than it used to be. Weeds may be invading the lawn; trees may be growing taller than you expected, blocking light to plants beneath them; flower beds may need thinning. In short, nature is taking its course.

The inset photographs *opposite* illustrate five common landscaping problems. Although these photographs were taken in the Midwest, the problems could occur in a wide range of climatic and geographical conditions.

1 Shrubs too close to the house. Roots can damage a home's foundations, and constant friction from branches can wear away a portion of the siding (or roof if they're tall enough). Branches and leaves that touch the structure steadily also can cause moisture damage. Pruning one side of the plants to create a passageway is one solution. Replanting a foot or so farther out—beyond the drip line from the eaves—is another. Keep in mind, however, that not all shrubs take kindly to transplanting.

2 Too much shade. On a hot, sunny day, you're likely to want all the shade around your house you can get, but lawn grasses and many other plants don't do well in heavy shade, so you may decide you need a little more sun. A costly and drastic solution to the problem is to remove an entire tree. If that's your choice, be sure the tree you plan to eliminate isn't a key landscaping feature that contributes more than you realize to the charm of your home and neighborhood. Skillful, heavy pruning may be a better solution in some instances. Or, you can choose to live with the shade, choosing low-light plants to

replace the struggling lawn. You also might consider installing a patio or deck in the shaded areas, to eliminate the problem of finding plants that thrive in shade.

3 Bare spots. These may result from too much shade, as in the inset *opposite.* Mulching around the tree can cover the bare spot, and help the ground around the tree retain moisture. Again, you can also experiment with shade-tolerant plantings.

4 Erosion. In the example pictured *opposite,* slope and lack of soil-holding roots caused earth to wash away. Sturdy plants that can tolerate some foot traffic can help; so can installing an edging in a trench beside the steps. Be sure foot traffic is limited as much as possible to the steps and paths to avoid trampling pathside plants.

5 Overgrown beds. If these are growing onto paths, cutting them back will solve the problem. Putting edging around mid-yard beds also will help contain them. If you're setting out new plantings along a path, be sure to allow several inches of empty space between the first row of plantings and the path. That way, when the plants reach full size, they won't overlap the walkway.

1 Shrubs too close to house.

2 Too much shade.

3 Bare spots.

4 Erosion.

5 Overgrown beds.

MAKING
A YARD
MANAGEABLE

The photograph *at right* shows the yard at our project house before we started work on it. Among the items that needed attention:

• The trees to the right of the house provided such dense shade that little could grow under them, resulting in unsightly bare spots like those pictured on page 25.

• The medium-size honey locust tree growing squarely in front of the house seemed awkward and out of place, and provided little shade.

• Even more serious than these problems was the branch overhanging the roof from the left. It was scraping against the roof and had worn away shingles and the building felt underneath. Moisture held by the leaves was beginning to rot the sheathing.

• Several low-growing trees

and evergreen shrubs were too close to foundation walls.

• The sloping area, visible in the left foreground, was starting to erode. In addition, the stone retaining wall above it was beginning to crumble, turning what should have been an attractive feature into a potentially hazardous eyesore.

• The lawn's overall condition needed improving. Weeds were starting to take over in several areas, and grass was sparse in others.

To handle the major overhauling chores, we hired a team of three professional landscapers. They completed their work in 1½ days, at a cost of $425 plus materials. For an in-depth look at what they did, see pages 28 and 29. For more about gardening services, see the box below.

(continued)

GARDENING SERVICES

The days of the willing and reliable kid next door who mows your lawn and rakes your leaves are over in most places. But in many regions, particularly in suburban areas, you can hire a professional gardening service—usually listed in the Yellow Pages under "Landscape Contractors"—to do as much or as little of the routine yard maintenance as you like.

Often a basic package includes regularly scheduled lawn mowing and seasonal tasks such as leaf clearing. Extra services include fertilizing, planting, sodding, pruning, even repairing

retaining walls. (To learn about firms that specialize in lawn care, see page 28.)

If you want someone to do a full-scale cleanup on a yard (as we did for our house), most gardening services will provide this kind of one-time assistance.

If you'd like a specific task done with professional skill, consider hiring a landscape contractor. Having a professional prune established shrubs that have been neglected may cost you well over a hundred dollars, but they'll look much better, and you'll be able to keep them in shape yourself for years afterward.

The inset photograph above shows our landscaping crew at work. One is pruning low-growing shrubs, one is trimming taller plants with lopping shears, and the third is mowing the lawn with a mini-tractor.

MAKING
A YARD
MANAGEABLE
(continued)

Here's what our project house looked like after some overdue maintenance chores were carried out. Much of the work won't have to be done again for several years; other tasks, if done regularly, should take considerably fewer hours than they did this time.

Here's a rundown of changes made in response to the problems identified on page 26.

• The trees to the right of the house were cut back. They still provide shade, but not as much; now there's enough sun filtering through the leaves to allow a low-maintenance, shade-tolerant ground cover to thrive. An edging strip (see pages 30 and 31 for more about edging) was put in to hold back the ground cover and simplify maintenance.

• To both the left and right of the house, several small trees as well as some shrubs were removed because they were growing too close to the foundation. The tree blocking the front door also was taken down, improving the home's appearance and easing front-step access.

• The overhanging branch that rubbed away roofing was removed. Look carefully at the left side of the roof and you can see the damage it did.

• The sod was removed from the sloping lawn in the left foreground and replaced by creeping junipers, which require minimal maintenance and hold soil very effectively. The rock retaining wall, which had been crumbling and threatened by erosion, was shored up.

• The rest of the lawn was handled two ways: Sections with good sod were cleaned up and weeded; those with sod in poor condition were patched with new sod.

LAWN SERVICES

Once a yard is in manageable condition, a professional gardening service, of the type discussed on page 26, may be more than you need. Even if you decide to do all routine maintenance chores yourself, however, you may decide your lawn needs professional help to get it green and lush.

Many national and regional chains, as well as local companies, offer lawn-care programs that include seeding, fertilization, and weed and insect control at regular intervals in the course of a year. These are typically listed in the Yellow Pages under "Lawn Maintenance." Although some also provide gardening services, their main function is to improve a lawn's overall health and appearance.

Many lawn services charge by the square foot. Many also have a minimum fee—$125 for a year's worth of treatments, for example. If this is the cost for a 5,000-square-foot lawn, you'll pay more per square foot for a 3,000-square-foot lawn than a neighbor with a larger one. It may be worth it, however, if you've already spent several years trying unsuccessfully to upgrade your lawn—or if you don't want to bother.

LAWN
KEEPING

Because lawn grasses come in so many varieties, each suited to certain soil, climatic, and geographical conditions, it's almost impossible to make a hard-and-fast schedule of lawn maintenance needs that applies to all lawns in all regions. Nevertheless, there are certain things you have to do no matter what type of lawn you have and no matter where you live.

Because it has to be done so often, mowing comes to mind first. A lawn that's allowed to grow too high won't thrive; neither will one that's cut too short. It could be vul-

nerable to damage, particularly early in the growing season. A general rule to follow is: Don't cut off more than you leave. For example, 2 inches is a good height for many types of grass, so ideally you should mow your lawn before—but not much before—it reaches a height of 4 inches. How long it takes for grass to reach that height between mowings depends on the season, soil conditions, and type of grass, among other factors.

Making mowing easier
The fewer obstacles there are on your lawn, the easier it will be to mow. A large, unbroken

expanse of lawn is considerably faster and easier to mow than two or three smaller, irregularly shaped lawn areas or a lawn broken up by nonmowable plantings.

When you come to the edge of a lawn, you may find yourself left with a narrow border of grass that doesn't seem to get cut as neatly as the rest of the lawn, or grass that's being invaded by neighboring ground cover and starting to look ragged. One way to simplify maintenance at these peripheral zones is to install a *mowing strip,* a 6- to 12-inch-wide border of concrete, wood, stone, or brick. The

border should be flush with the ground.

The drawing below shows how mowing strips can simplify a mowing plan. Note that the strips run perpendicular to the mower's path.

An *edging trench* is another possibility. An edging trench gives you more room to maneuver and separates the lawn from other plantings. To keep aggressive ground covers away from the lawn, consider using *edging strips.*

For more about edging strips and edging tools, see the captions below and photographs *opposite.*

(continued)

MOWING PLAN

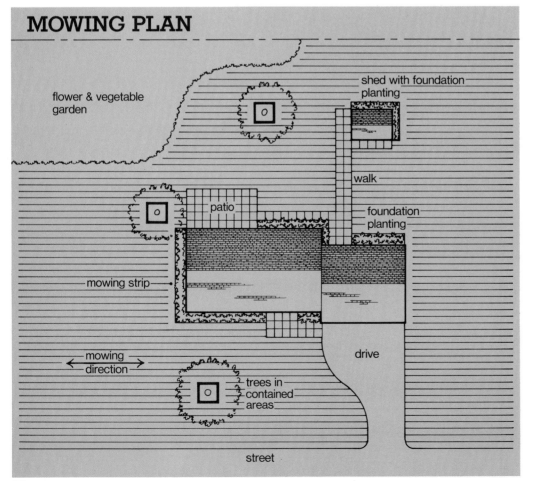

flower & vegetable garden

shed with foundation planting

walk

foundation planting

patio

mowing strip

mowing direction

drive

trees in contained areas

street

Edging strips, like the ones pictured opposite, offer a tidy way to separate your lawn from other planting areas. Here's a rundown of the major types.
• **TREATED FIR** works well when it's sunk into the ground. It usually needs no staking, but may heave periodically.
• **REDWOOD BENDER BOARD** negotiates curves. It must be secured to stakes with brass or galvanized screws.
• **VINYL**—either solid as shown here, or metal-capped—can be sunk into the ground without staking and flexes more easily than bender board.
• **METAL** is the most expensive and permanent material. Pieces interlock at stakes, which makes this edging difficult to cut. Don't use metal adjacent to concrete; rusting can cause stains.

TREATED FIR

REDWOOD BENDER BOARD

VINYL

METAL

The tools pictured at right can help you create and maintain clean edges.

• GAS-POWERED EDGER. This digs for you, tossing clods of grass and earth to the side. Quieter, less powerful electric edgers also are available.

• HAND-OPERATED ROLLING EDGER. The principle is the same as for a power edger, but you supply the energy.

• SPADE. This might be described as a foot-powered edger. A square-nose spade, not shown, also is effective for edging.

• GRASS EDGER. This machine trims narrow boundary areas.

LAWN KEEPING

(continued)

Devices to help you apply pesticides and herbicides come in many shapes and sizes. The wick in the foreground of the photograph below does spot work; the various sprayers allow you to cover large areas. Choose a sprayer that suits both the material you're using and the area you want to cover.

Good maintenance reduces your lawn's vulnerability to pests and disease. If you mow your lawn on schedule and water it to a depth of 6 to 12 inches during hot, dry weather, the grass will stay reasonably healthy and look presentable throughout much of the growing season. If you also feed it and follow a few basic rules, it will look even better.

Fertilizing
Timely and appropriate feeding—either with chemical fertilizer or organic materials such as sludge, cottonseed meal,

screened compost, and well-rotted manure—is one of the keys to a thriving lawn. Exactly when and how to fertilize your lawn depends largely on where you live. Generally, however, you should feed the lawn in spring and again in late summer or early fall. (In the South, spring or early summer is the best time for fertilizing lawns; in the North, fall is considered best.)

In cool wet weather, you can apply both types of fertilizer without any aftercare. If you use chemical fertilizer for your lawn's late-summer feeding,

however, be sure to water the lawn afterward so the chemicals don't burn the grass. (Organic fertilizers are slower-acting and don't burn grass.)

Getting rid of weeds is another almost-inevitable maintenance task. The best time to weed is when you're doing other yard work, such as seeding and fertilizing.

Weeds and disease
There are several approaches to take to weed control. First, regular mowing keeps weeds from going to seed, and you can dig out isolated weeds. If your lawn has so many unwel-

come plants growing on it that digging is inefficient, you will probably have to turn to chemical and organic methods of controlling weeds. Selective weedkillers are available, so identify the weeds and determine the best method for getting rid of them.

If you decide to use a chemical herbicide on your lawn, be very careful. Not only can chemicals pollute the air, soil, and water, but they also can damage the grass and retard the growth of new seed.

Leaf-bagging machines, like the one shown below, left, act like outdoor vacuum cleaners. Many lawn mowers also come with a leaf-bagging attachment. If you prefer raking, a bag cart like the one shown below, right, helps you move the bag and keep it open while you stuff it.

Diseases are another hazard many lawns face. Among the most common are fungus diseases. One of the best ways to avoid these is to water your lawn during the day, so the grass has a chance to dry by nightfall: Grass that stays wet for a long time provides an ideal environment for fungus diseases. If you think your lawn is suffering from a disease, try to identify it with the help of an illustrated gardening book and follow the recommended treatment, or consult a professional.

Beyond the basics
Besides fertilizing and weeding, you'll need to do some thatching and spot-reseeding each year. Garden books and other sources offer an abundance of advice about techniques, materials, and frequency.

If your lawn has many bare or weedy patches, you may have to make a new lawn. First, be sure the soil is ready: It must be graded, tested, and cultivated before being planted or sodded. Also, the soil should be fertilized in advance, and weed- and insect-free.

Seeding is probably the most common way to start a lawn. In a cool climate where grasses do well, it's also the most economical. *Sprigging* uses grass sprigs that are really pieces of stem taken from the sod; *stolonizing,* a variation on sprigging, broadcasts sprigs by the bushel. *Plugging* uses small sections of sod; it's frequently done in the South. *Sodding* is a highly popular but expensive option. It's a good choice where seeding is difficult or where you want results in a hurry.

For more about establishing a regular yard-maintenance agenda that includes lawn upkeep, see pages 36 and 37.

MULCHING AND COMPOSTING

Just because leaves must be removed from your lawn doesn't mean you have to discard them. Shredded or whole, they provide an acceptable mulch around the base of shrubs. Leaves not only help the soil retain moisture and help moderate changes in soil temperature, but, as they age, they also return valuable nutrients to the soil.

You can carry organic enrichment of soil a step further by using the leaves you collect each autumn as a major component of a compost heap. Basically, *compost* is a collection of well-decomposed organic materials; in addition to leaves, it can include trimmings from healthy plants and dead plants you would usually spade under when

you're working in the garden. Compost makes both an excellent mulch and a good soil conditioner, but it's not a substitute for a balanced fertilizer, especially in a new garden or one that has not been regularly conditioned with compost or other types of humus.

SPAS, HOT TUBS, AND SWIMMING POOLS

A spa, hot tub, or swimming pool is a delightful amenity, and a major responsibility. All require similar, conscientious maintenance. You must keep the water itself clean and safe, free of bacteria, algae, and foreign objects such as leaves. You also have to keep the facility's shell clean and take care of vital equipment, such as filters, pumps, and drains. Because sizes, materials, and water temperatures vary, however, the specifics of maintenance have to be adjusted accordingly.

Keeping the water clean
To prevent bacteria and algae growth in spa, hot tub, and pool water, you need chemicals and other control systems. Because hot tubs and spas use hot water, which provides excellent growing conditions for bacteria and algae, they require more frequent maintenance than swimming pools.
• *Chlorine* is the chemical most widely used to disinfect water. The form that's usually recommended for use in spas and hot tubs is a powder called sodium dichlor. Liquids and tablets, as well as powders, are used in home pools. Chlorine attacks bacteria and algae and is neutralized in the process; some remains free in the water to work as needed.
• *Bromine* also is used to purify water. It works in much the same way as chlorine but does not evaporate as fast, smell as strong, or irritate eyes to the same extent. Iodine is sometimes used to purify pools, too.

You'll need a test kit to determine how much of a chemical is left in the water at a given time, and how much more you must add. No matter what chemical you use, be sure to follow package instructions to the letter to avoid injury to yourself and damage to the pool or tub materials.

Keeping water chemically balanced
Besides being clean, the water must be chemically balanced so it's neither too acid nor too alkaline. Water that's too alkaline leaves a residue on the tub or pool, clouds the water, irritates eyes, and keeps purifying agents from working at top efficiency. Water that's too acid corrodes pipes and some linings, stains other materials, makes disinfectants dissipate too fast, and irritates eyes.

Water's chemical balance is measured on a pH scale that ranges from 0 to 14; 7 is neutral. The water in your recreational facility should be slightly alkaline—between about 7.2 and 7.6. To make water less acid, add sodium bicarbonate (soda ash); to make it less alkaline, add an acid, such as sodium bisulfate (dry acid) to a spa or hot tub and liquid muriatic acid to a pool. These chemicals, like disinfectants, come with detailed instructions for safe and effective use.

Maintenance tips
In addition to maintaining the proper chemical conditions, you have to keep water free of contaminants you can see. This breaks down into several tasks requiring specific tools.
• To get rid of leaves, use a leaf skimmer, a metal or plastic frame with a mesh net attached.

• Clean the hot tub, spa, or pool's liner or walls with rags, sponges, and special-purpose nylon brushes.
• Remove debris from the bottom of the facility with a vacuum cleaner, one that's built into the pool filtration system or an independent jet cleaner that connects to a garden hose. Automatic pool cleaners replace vacuum cleaners and brushes; both built-in and portable types are available.

Behind the scenes
Because a hot tub, spa, or pool is not regulated by nature, as ponds and lakes are, they also have mechanical equipment that requires care. Make sure filters are clear of debris and backwash them as recommended by the manufacturer.

Pumps and motors usually need minimal maintenance, but read all the materials that came with them; they may need periodic lubrication. Be sure, too, that a pool's pump strainer is clean before and after vacuuming (and, if you have a sand filter, before and after backwashing as well).

Seasonal care
If you live in a cold climate, you probably won't be using your pool, tub, or spa for at least half of the year. During this period, the facility will need little maintenance; you may choose to cover a pool or to drain it. Covering a spa, pool, or tub keeps off falling leaves and maintains a tidy look during the off-season. You will probably be happier with the appearance of a porous cover. These allow rainwater to pass through, eliminating accumulations of unsightly dirty water that could cause a waterproof cover to sag.

DEVELOPING YOUR OWN YARD MAINTENANCE AGENDA

Just as one organization's business or economic agenda is bound to differ from another's, so does every homeowner's agenda differ in some way from that of the people next door. The differences are the result of several factors.

Clearly, the size and complexity of your yard will determine what goes on your agenda. If you have a small lawn, a flowering ornamental tree, and two evergreen shrubs, for example, your maintenance chores are bound to be simple, no matter how high your standards. If you have a larger area and a greater variety of plantings, your maintenance agenda becomes a matter of priorities and interests, as well as available time and money.

Where you live makes a big difference, too. If you live in a cold climate—what some call a four-season zone—you already know certain types of plants won't do well because

they're not hardy. If you live with year-round spring and summer, you also face some limitations, although with different species and for different reasons. The climate does more than affect what you can grow, however; it also affects the rhythm of your work. You can't cultivate frozen ground, for example, and you may want to avoid strenuous work in hot weather.

Setting standards

The standards you set for your home also help determine your specific agenda. It's safe to assume you want your yard to look attractive and reasonably well cared-for, but that's just a starting point. Do you want your lawn to be a showpiece? Would you like to have a seasonal display of flowers that the whole neighborhood makes a point of walking or driving past? Do you want to establish a low-maintenance yard? One where children can play freely?

Once you've identified the extent of care you want to lavish on—or dole out to—your yard, it's time to sit down and make a list of things to do. The basic yard-maintenance tasks are watering, weeding, and fertilizing. Mulching, staking, controlling pests, and installing new plants of whatever type are important activities, too. How often you carry out the various tasks and the proportion of your time each requires depends on what you have and on what you want to accomplish. Perhaps the most efficient way to figure it out is to divide your yard into care zones, such as lawns, trees, shrubs, flower beds, ground covers, and so on.

Lawns and ground covers

Every lawn needs to be mowed throughout its growing season. Whether you do it once a week or every other

week depends on how fast it grows and how manicured you want it to look. Grass needs cutting less often in hot weather because it grows much more slowly then—and is also more vulnerable to damage from the mower.

It's hard to be precise about how often a lawn should be watered. If you live where there's usually very little rain during the growing season, you'll not only have to find plant materials that can tolerate local conditions, you also may have to contend with local water-use restrictions. If you do water your lawn, do it regularly and deeply, so the roots can develop properly.

If you decide not to water your lawn during a hot, dry spell in the Northeast, it will brown off, but revive when cool, moist weather returns. In the Southwest, you don't have this option—you must water the lawn or it will die.

Fertilizing needs to be done once or twice a year; when depends on where you live. Similarly, most lawns need partial renewal each year. There's almost always a bare spot to reseed, resod, or fill.

Ground covers can save you some lawn-maintenance tasks. They spread readily, hold the soil, cover awkward angles and slopes, and come in many varieties, which in turn tolerate a wide range of conditions. If, for example, you plant a sturdy, shade-resistant ground cover on a tree-shaded slope, you will save yourself the trouble of trying to make grass grow where it isn't really comfortable. Ground cover is more than a coverup, though; it's a landscaping feature in its own right and needs some attention to keep looking its best.

Most common ground covers, such as periwinkle, pachysandra, and ivy, are resistant to disease, and because they grow densely, they discourage competition from weeds. Some do need control, though—cutting back or digging up is the basic maintenance for aggressive ground covers.

Trees and shrubs
Trees and shrubs are what give most yards their individuality. They are also the source of a variety of maintenance chores. Deciduous trees drop their leaves during the dormant season; that means raking. Some varieties also shed seed pods, blossoms, and sap, all of which contribute further to cleanup chores. For well-established trees, you probably will have to build these tasks into your maintenance schedule. If you're planning to add trees, choose neat varieties—ones with small leaves and no messy fruit or blossoms.

Mature trees don't often need pruning; when they do, it's usually a job for a professional. Shrubs are another matter, however: Regular pruning is vital to their health and appearance. Shrubs are not all meant to be pruned at the same time of year—some need to be trimmed in winter, others at the end of the growing season. Some evergreens require special treatment. Check on the requirements for your shrubs before you do anything.

Flowers and vegetables
Flowers make taking care of your yard fun. You can go to a local garden center in late spring and buy several flats of low-maintenance annuals, set them out, do nothing more than water and occasionally weed the area around them, and have a lovely flower bed for one season. You can plant bulbs and have a delightful display of color for several springs, with almost no additional effort. Or you can plant a stand of daylilies that almost never needs weeding or watering, yet comes back into rewarding flower each summer.

Once you decide you want flowers around the house, you need to establish a watering and weeding schedule; frequency depends on the weather and the vigor of your weeds. Mulching keeps down weeds to some extent and helps the soil around the flowers retain water, but it won't eliminate the need to do some work.

Vegetables are another optional yard feature. If you have a vegetable garden in your yard, you are, of course, adding to your maintenance schedule. It must be planned, planted, watered, weeded, staked, and protected from hungry insects and animals. As with flowers, mulching and good planning—taking care, for example, to plant varieties known to do well in your area—will help, but there's no substitute for work when it comes to raising vegetables.

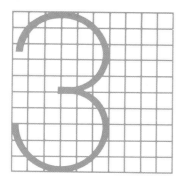

YOUR HOME'S EXTERIOR

Maintaining a home's outside surfaces is a never-ending job, but one that you can eventually whittle down and get better at. In the early years of owning a home—especially if it's an older one—you may have to invest time and money getting things into a more easily maintainable shape. The payback comes later, as you develop a maintenance program that gets on top of small problems before they become big ones. This chapter covers a home's exterior, from foundation to chimney top, and offers pointers to help you with your own exterior maintenance agenda.

IDENTIFYING EXTERIOR PROBLEMS

From the street or a neighbor's backyard, the exterior of our project house looks presentable. On closer inspection, though, we found many small maintenance problems that, if put off any longer, could soon lead to big trouble. That's why any homeowner should keep track of exterior wear and tear with a semi-annual inspection tour. All you need are the few simple tools listed in the box at right and a checklist of potential trouble spots.

Start at the bottom by systematically examining the foundation and basement window wells. Next, take a careful look at siding and corner joints, window and door trim, sills, drip caps, and the windows and doors themselves. Finally, turn your gaze upward to assess the condition of gutters and downspouts, soffits and fascia, roofing, attic vents, and flashings. These are the basics. Add to your list features unique to your house, such as shutters, porch railings, or solar heating devices.

Exterior deterioration shows up in many forms but isn't difficult to spot, even if this is your first season as a homeowner. Some problems, such as a leaf-clogged gutter, a finger-thick crack in a foundation, or a missing roof shingle, are obvious. More subtle signs show up as discoloration, unexpected stains, crumbling mortar, blistering paint, cracked siding, or damaged roofing.

Our inspection tour turned up problems in many of these areas. Clearly, we had some patching work ahead to restore our project house to an easily maintainable state. Come along and see what we found, and what we did.

A DETECTIVE KIT FOR TRACKING EXTERIOR PROBLEMS

Before you set out on an exterior inspection tour, assemble a few simple tools. Here are the items to bring along.
- A *flashlight* beam ferrets out problems in the darkness of a basement window well or a soffit on the sunless north side of a house.
- A *paint scraper* drawn over what appears to be loose paint tells you quickly if it is indeed loose.
- A *screwdriver* poked and scratched along mortar joints identifies loose mortar that needs repointing.
- A *penknife* blade, gently probed at caulked joints, indicates whether caulking is still flexible. If it's dry and crumbling, you'll need to recaulk.
- *Binoculars* enable you to look at a roof without climbing around on it. It's a good idea to stay off any roof—not only because of the danger of falling but also because you could damage roofing materials. To get a close look at a roof, view it through field glasses from a ladder raised to eave level. (See page 46 for tips about using ladders.)

Also bring along a pencil and paper so you can list any problems you find.

1 Any break in siding leaks heat and invites seepage. Here a piece of clapboard has warped and split. Also check for leaks around service line entry points, such as the conduit ell at the top of the photograph. To learn about repairing damaged siding, see page 50. Seal around penetrations with caulking.

2 This joint between window trim and a sill shows the damage that can be wrought by prolonged exposure to weather, especially where drainage is slow. Once paint is gone, wood rot begins. The remedy: Scrape away loose paint, reprime, caulk, and repaint.

3 Soffits and the undersides of gutters, always in shadow, retain moisture. As a result, these surfaces often lose paint faster than sun-dried areas. Scrape, reprime, and paint bare spots.

4 Pay special attention to flashings—leakproofing metal sheet goods laid in joints between unlike materials. Here flashing is pulling away from the chimney and needs to be sealed with roofing cement.

5 Flashing around any roof penetration, such as this vent pipe, is subject to movement from temperature changes, and movement opens cracks. Again, patch with roofing cement. Notice that the shingles on our house are beginning to curl and have lost much of their granule coating. This roof isn't going to last much longer.

1 Breaks in siding.

2 Sill damage.

3 Peeling soffits and gutters.

4 Deteriorated chimney flashing.

5 Deteriorated vent flashing.

KEEPING OUT WEATHER

Here, a shingle that strong winds lifted and warped is sealed down with dabs of roofing cement. Apply the cement beneath left and right shingle edges; for three-tab shingles, apply cement in the middle, too.

If sheet metal flashing around a chimney is in good condition but pulling loose, clean the area and re-cement the nearest row of shingles to the base flashing (the part that's flat against the roof deck). If the flashing is damaged, call in a professional.

Rain, sleet, snow, sun, and wind beat relentlessly on a home's exterior. Roofs take the brunt of it, but siding, windows and doors, foundations, and other outside elements all suffer at nature's hands. Ignore its ravages and small cracks soon become big ones. Once that happens, it doesn't take long for a leak to wreck interior surfaces, ruin furnishings and equipment, and even threaten a home's structure.

Use sealants as your first line of defense against weather. A few cans of roofing cement and several tubes of caulking can forestall hundreds, even thousands, of dollars in repair bills.

Getting around on a roof
You don't need a lot of talent to wield a putty knife or caulking gun. In fact, the hardest part about sealing jobs is getting to them. Roofs pose a special problem because, as noted earlier in this chapter, walking around on a roof can damage it.

Usually it's possible to reach a roof's lower regions from a ladder propped against a side of the house. If you have to make a repair higher up on a slope, firmly fasten a long, strong rope to the top rung of a straight ladder. Lean the ladder against one side of the house, then maneuver the rope across the roof's ridge and down the other side of the house. Raise the ladder so that it lies flat on the roof alongside the area you want to repair.

Now, pull the rope taut and fasten it around a tree trunk, car bumper, or other secure mooring. With a second ladder, climb to the roof and make your way to the damaged spot along the rungs of the ladder on the roof.

Because your weight is distributed along the entire length of the ladder, you minimize the pressure any one shingle has to bear.

Repairing roofs
The photographs above show three repairs that had to be made to our asphalt shingle roof. Wood shingles, wood shakes, and slate are approached differently. Instead of gluing or sealing, you need to replace any faulty shingle,

Raindrops can course under an unprotected eave and generate rot in soffits. A drip edge—pictured above both installed and **loose—lets drops fall to the gutter or ground. A bead of roofing cement holds the lowest course of shingles to the drip edge.**

The header or drip cap over windows and doors diverts rain—until cracks open at the siding/header joint. Then water seeps behind **the trim and into the wall around the frame. A bead of caulking (see the box below) seals the joint, preventing rot.**

shake, or slate. To do this, slip a hacksaw blade beneath the broken shingle and cut through the two roofing nails holding it. Slide out the defective shingle and clean the roofing paper underneath. Then, gently tap a new shingle beneath the course above until the butt end is level with its own course. Finally, nail just below the line of the course above (drill holes through slate before you nail it), and seal the nailheads with roofing cement.

Repairs to built-up (flat or nearly flat) roofing, copper, terne metal, and clay tile generally are best handled by professionals. *(continued)*

CHOOSING THE RIGHT SEALANT

Dissimilar materials expand and contract at different rates, which explains why cracks so often appear at joints between metal and wood, masonry and asphalt shingles, and other unlike building materials. Caulking bridges these gaps by remaining flexible over years of temperature changes.

Shop for caulking and you'll find a wide range of choices. Oil-based caulks, the least expensive, hold up for only a year or so. Steer away from latex-based caulks, too; they're best limited to indoor situations.

Acrylic copolymers, butyls, and silicone-based compounds all work well outdoors. For general caulking jobs, choose a moderately priced acrylic copolymer. Butyl, which costs more, is exceptionally good for sealing seams in gutters and for metal-to-masonry joints. Silicone caulking, the most expensive, is also the most durable and can be used almost anywhere.

Before you buy caulking, read label directions carefully. Paint won't adhere to some silicone formulations, for example. Other caulks are paintable once they've cured, a process that takes up to 48 hours. Instead of painting a caulk, you might use a pretinted one. You also can buy clear, colorless caulks; these typically cloud slightly after several years.

KEEPING OUT WEATHER
(continued)

WEATHER-STRIPPING OPTIONS

	LOCATION	INSTALLATION
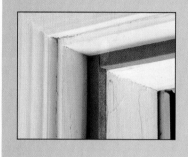 **FOAM** Cellular strips of foam—rubber, vinyl, or urethane—with adhesive applied on one side and protected with paper.	Don't apply foam where it's subject to friction. The material won't survive. This limits it to swinging doors, the tops and bottoms of double-hung windows, and other compression-only situations.	Easiest of all. Measure the length needed; snip with scissors. Strip away the backing paper and press the adhesive side into place.
 **BULB OR BEAD** Vinyl tubing, hollow or filled with foam vinyl, attached to a wide flange. The flange may be all vinyl or reinforced with aluminum.	Apply anywhere around windows, including meeting rails, and around doors except at thresholds, where you may need a sweep or other specialized weather lock.	Cut all-vinyl strips with scissors, the aluminum-reinforced type with snips. At 8-inch intervals, tack down the vinyl flange so that the bead or bulb presses against gaps between stationary and moving parts. The aluminum-reinforced type has predrilled holes for nailing.
 **SPRING METAL** Generally aluminum, sometimes brass. V-shape in cross section. One leg of the V attaches to the frame; the window or door compresses the other leg.	Same as for bulb or bead.	Most spring metal strips have predrilled holes. Tack through them. Make certain the bottom of the V faces a closing entry door. For all window types, the bottom of the V faces the weather side. Cut with snips.
 **INTERLOCKING METAL** Generally aluminum, sometimes brass. Two strips, each J-shape, attach separately to the door and frame, and interlock when the door is closed.	Use only around swinging doors and casement windows.	Carefully align the interlocking metal strips so that the Js fit snugly into one another. The bottom of the J on the moving part should face inside. Cut with snips; tack through predrilled holes.

EFFECTIVENESS	COST
Befitting its low cost, foam weather stripping may begin to deteriorate when it passes the first year of service. Because of its closed-cell foam structure, the strip blocks air well.	Inexpensive
Because this flexible vinyl strip is solid, it lasts much longer than foam. Aluminum-reinforced vinyl has been known to survive for two decades. When installed properly, the vinyl bead stops air loss, but you may not like the look of the visible flange.	Moderate; moderately expensive with aluminum reinforcing.
Spring metal lasts a long time and plugs air leaks well. Because metal is the worst of insulators, however, you can expect some minor heat loss by conductance.	Moderate
Nothing beats interlocking metal as a barrier to air infiltration. Installed so the strips fit together smoothly, this type is virtually permanent. Like spring metal, it can conduct small amounts of house heat to the outdoors.	Expensive

GLAZING BASICS

If you've ever tried to hire someone to replace a single broken windowpane, you know why learning how to do it yourself makes sense. Even if you can coax a handyman over for a small job, you end up paying a premium in labor charges. Here's what to do.

Start by clearing the way for the new glass. Carefully remove any remaining shards of glass and scrape off all old glazing compound from wood or steel windows. In the sash channel you'll find little triangular glazing points or, in metal windows, spring clips; remove these. With aluminum windows, a gasket holds the glass in place; pull this out with needle-nose pliers.

Measuring and cutting

Now measure the sash opening at several points along the length and width (not all sash frames are perfectly square). Reduce the two measurements by 1/16 inch, so the new pane will slip into the opening without jamming. It's easiest to have the pane precut for you at a hardware store, but you can buy a large sheet of glass and cut from it the pane you need.

To cut the glass yourself, first lay it on a flat, even surface and mark the measurements you made with a crayon or felt-tip pen.

Use a steel straightedge to guide the glass cutter, a metal handle about the size of a pencil with a hardened steel wheel at the working end. Apply moderate pressure on the wheel to score the glass surface from edge to edge. Now position the scored line just over a table edge, allowing the part that you don't want to hang over. Hold the glass firmly against the table and, with the heel of your other hand, sharply rap the unwanted part. The glass will break roughly along the scored line. Use the cutter to snip away any jagged edges, or use a pair of pliers.

Installing the glass

If your sash is wood, coat the groove with linseed oil to prevent dry wood from drawing off oil in the glazing compound. This isn't required for steel.

To install the pane in a wood or steel sash, first lay a thin coat of glazing compound in the sash channel and press the pane into this soft layer. With wood windows, gently press in two glazier's points per side to hold the glass. With steel windows, use spring clips. With your fingers, lay in glazing compound and smooth it with an oil-lubricated putty knife. When the compound dries, paint it to match the sash.

To install glass in an aluminum sash, buy a new vinyl gasket and force it into the groove around the glass with a putty knife.

Straight ladder

Extension ladder

Platform ladder

Stepladder

Trestle ladder

EXTERIOR HOUSEKEEPING

Just as the inside of a house periodically needs to be cleaned and spruced up, so does its exterior. Dirty windows begin to make the view outside look dingy. Leaves and other debris collect in gutters. Chimneys cake with soot.

One of the most important tools for keeping up the exterior of a house is a secure ladder. The photograph *opposite* shows five ways to extend your reach. A *platform ladder* is highly portable and can be used indoors as well. *Straight* and *extension ladders* get you to high places. A *stepladder* is an all-around, indoor/outdoor workhorse. A *trestle ladder* can serve as a straight ladder, a stepladder, or—by folding it as shown and laying planks across the top—a scaffold.

Wood ladders are the least expensive and the heaviest. Aluminum and magnesium ladders are lightweight and moderately costly. *(continued)*

LADDER SAFETY TIPS

1 Set a ladder on solid, level ground. Shim only with a nonslip support, such as a concrete block.

2 Climb only to the next-to-the-top step on a stepladder; on a straight or extension ladder, stop at a rung that puts your shoulder even with the top.

3 Raise the movable half of an extension ladder only to its safety mark.

4 Lean a ladder against a house so that the distance from the foundation to the ladder's base is about one-quarter of its height.

HOW TO SQUEEGEE WINDOWS

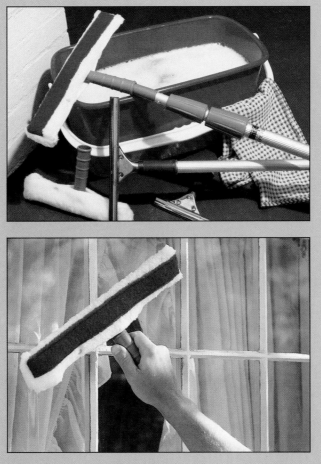

With the tools shown here, you can clean windows like a pro. Clockwise from lower left are: a lamb's wool or fabric scrubber; a combination sponge and lamb's wool scrubber; a wide basin for easy dipping; soft, absorbent cloths; a narrow squeegee for small windowpanes; and a wide squeegee. An extension pole reaches high windows.

Soaked with detergent-sudsy water, the combination scrubber makes quick work of cleaning windows. You also can use it on siding, shutters, or just about any other outside surface. Use the sponge side to spread suds, the fabric side to scrub. Then give the washed surface a fresh-water rinse, using the medium-spray setting on a hose nozzle.

You can dry windows much faster with a squeegee than with rags or paper towels. The main trick is to wipe the squeegee blade after each swipe across wet glass. If the rubber blade is wet, it will skip some of the surface water on the next stroke. Pull the blade smoothly from top to bottom; then wipe water from the bottom muntin.

EXTERIOR HOUSEKEEPING
(continued)

Remove as many leaves from a gutter as you can by hand, then flush the residue down the spout with water from a hose. If a spout stops up or seems sluggish, direct a high-pressure stream of water into it.

Inspect galvanized steel gutters for rust, aluminum for powdery white oxidation. Get rid of either by wire-brushing and finishing up with steel wool. Prepare the area for recoating (see below). If gutters aren't protected with screen guards, install them.

Gutters and downspouts also require frequent attention. Check them twice a year, in spring and late fall. Clear away any debris you find, and look for signs of rusting or other deterioration.

To clean gutters you'll need work gloves, a bucket for the debris, and a garden hose. To minimize ladder-moving, also make yourself a gutter rake by attaching an L-bracket to one end of a long 1x2. Set up the ladder near the center of a gutter run, then rake leaves and other debris toward you from either direction.

As you clean, assess the condition of each gutter ele-ment. Are the hangers secure-ly attached? Do gutters slope slightly toward their outlets? As you hose out a gutter, notice what happens to the water. Standing water indicates that a gutter is sagging. Usually you can cure this by tightening the nearest hanger or installing a new one.

Check the downspouts, too. Sections should be securely fastened to each other and to the house. Where does water exiting the spout go? If you have splash blocks, they should be pitched away from foundation walls. If they're not, raise them and shim under-neath with gravel or sand.

REPAIRING METAL GUTTERS

Repainting is one way to seal a trouble spot that you've cleaned. First wash and rinse the area, and let it dry. On relatively new gal-vanized steel, dab the area with vinegar, rinse with wa-ter, and dry. Next, apply a coat of zinc-oxide primer to steel, or a primer specifical-ly designated for the metal.

Paint primed steel and clean aluminum with a metal topcoat. When that dries, apply a second coat.

• To fill a small hole in metal, clean the area around the hole. Then apply and smooth over the hole with a liquid steel or alumi-num (sold in a tube). Allow the patch to cure. Then prime and paint over the spot as explained above.
• To patch a large hole, fol-low the same steps, but cover and temporarily tape a piece of screening or fiberglass over the hole before applying the tube material.

Chimneys need regular inspections, too. While you're on the roof, check the condition of mortar joints and the chimney's cap. The inside of a chimney—its flue—deserves attention, too. Accumulated soot and, especially, creosote could cause a chimney to smoke or even catch fire.

If you frequently use a wood stove attached to your chimney or use your fireplace almost nightly in winter, have the chimney cleaned before every heating season, if not more often. If you use your fireplace less regularly, 20 or 30 times between November and March, for example, cleaning the chimney every two years should be sufficient.

Chimney cleaning is a task best left to professionals, not so much because of the skill it requires but because it's messy work. Not all professional sweeps arrive dressed in formal attire, but they do bring along the specialized equipment needed to clean the chimney flue thoroughly and to vacuum up soot. A pro also can assess the condition of your chimney's flue liner and advise you of any potentially dangerous condition, such as a cracked or broken flue tile.

With the increased popularity of wood stoves and heat-efficient fireplaces, chimney sweeps are easier to find. Check your community's Yellow Pages, and get recommendations from friends and neighbors.

With a protective tarp laid down, this sweep is putting soot into a paper bag. After most of the soot is bagged, he'll vacuum up the rest.

WHEN MATERIALS BREAK DOWN

As you probably already know, small flaws in your home's exterior materials soon become big ones. For example, a split clapboard invites water seepage. After water penetrates the wood, freeze-thaw cycles widen the split and eventually the board needs replacing. Other types of siding also can suffer damage. Here's what to do when materials break down.

• Replace a broken wood siding shingle the same way you would one on a roof. See page 42 to learn how.

• A scratch on aluminum siding disappears with a few strokes of acrylic or vinyl paint in a matching color. The same is true for vinyl siding, although you will probably have trouble even seeing a scratch on vinyl because the color goes all the way through.

• To seal a small puncture in aluminum siding, use a plasticized aluminum patcher. When the patch cures, sand, clean the area, and touch it up with metal paint.

• Close a tiny hole in vinyl with an acrylic latex caulk in a matching color.

• Large rips in aluminum or vinyl siding mean pieces must be replaced, which is not an easy job. You may do best to call in a contractor. If you decide to tackle the project yourself, gently pry up the course above the torn panel. To do this, you may have to remove the corner cap first. Pry out the nails along the top of the damaged panel and slip it out. Fit in the new section and nail through prepunched holes until nailheads barely meet the panel surface. Bend down the panel above.

Repair wood lap siding as shown and explained *at right*.

The best thing to do with a damaged corner cap, like the one shown here, is to replace it. Carefully remove the nails and the cap. If the siding underneath is also crushed, cut it off with a backsaw. Now cut a sliver from a new piece of siding and glue it in place with waterproof glue. Tap a new corner cap into position beneath the course above and nail it. Countersink the nailheads, caulk over them, and repaint.

When siding is this badly damaged, the entire board should be replaced. With a pry bar, carefully lift the board above, then tap it down again. Nails will pop out. Pull them, using a claw hammer and pry bar as shown. After all of the nails are pulled, remove the damaged board. If you find any tears in the building paper underneath, patch them with roofing cement. Cut a new board to fit snugly, slip it into place, and secure it with aluminum nails. Caulk the nailheads, prime, and paint.

When your palm comes up chalky after you've rubbed it along painted siding, the siding is chalking and due for a wash. Although not a serious condition, chalking dulls siding. Scrubbing with a flexible-bristle brush, household liquid detergent, and water, followed by a water rinse, will restore the siding's appearance. Shown here is a special hose attachment that speeds the job. A reservoir in the handle holds detergent or mildewcide.

What looks like chalk on brick facing is efflorescence, the natural result of salts leaching out of brick through evaporation. Clean off efflorescence with a commercial product or blend one part muriatic acid with 10 parts water. Wearing rubber gloves and protective glasses, dip a wire brush into the mix and scrub away the salts.

REMOVING OLD PAINT

When paint starts to peel, alligator (wrinkle), or blister, there's only one cure: Remove the old paint, sand, wash, prime, and repaint.

Before you begin, try to find out why the paint is deteriorating. Usually, evaporating moisture is the culprit. Fine vapor, working its way from the inside, pushes through the siding, taking off a few molecules of paint on each trip. Two possible remedies: Install a vent fan at the source of the moisture (a bath or laundry area, for example), or paint the inside walls with a vapor-barrier paint.

Scraping, wire-brushing, and sanding off grubby paint are laborious tasks. Here are four faster ways to remove paint.

• *Chemical strippers* are plentiful on paint store shelves. Some are toxic, however, so follow directions carefully.

• An *electric paint softener,* drawn across the surface, softens paint enough to push off the old coat with a wide-blade putty knife.

• A *propane torch* with a spreader tip does the same job as an electric softener. But be careful: You can set fire to a house with a torch.

• *Sandblasting* removes paint from masonry and stucco, but it's not a do-it-yourself project.

Repainting a wood-sided house is a big job that must be done every five to eight years. First, wash off chalking (see the previous page), then wire-brush or scrape off small patches of loose paint. For best results, apply a high-quality alkyd primer, then a good acrylic latex finish coat. Paint with a brush, as shown above, or roller, pad, or airless spray equipment.

MAINTAINING FINISHES

SIDING FINISHES

TYPE	SCHEDULED MAINTENANCE	TOUCH-UP MAINTENANCE
PAINTED SIDING	Inspect painted siding at least once a year. Look for minor signs of wear, such as dirty or chalking surfaces (see page 51). Pay close attention to more serious signs of paint failure, for which spot-scraping, sanding, and repainting may be necessary. Mildew can sometimes be a problem, especially low on a sidewall close to rising ground moisture. It looks like dirt at first glance, but look again and you'll see it as moist black or gray splotches.	Replace faulty boards as explained on page 50. Use the paint originally applied to the siding if possible. Dab a few strokes alongside the painted surface and let it dry; then see if new and old coats match. You may have to lighten old paint. If you're buying new paint, have the clerk match flakes you've removed from the siding. To avoid mildew in the future, buy paint with a mildewcide, or mix a mildewcide into the paint you have.
METAL SIDING	Spend 30 minutes once a year checking the state of aluminum or steel siding. On its surface, you may find some discoloration due to dirt, or dullness brought on by chalking. A water hose-down usually gets rid of this. If not, scrub with detergent; then rinse. Look, too, for dents. Sometimes, the dent will flatten out if you push it gently several times. If not, follow the guidelines at right.	Touch up a scratch on steel siding with a metal primer and acrylic latex finish coat; on aluminum siding you need only the finish coat. To match the existing siding color, mix a small amount of paint in a separate, clean container. Repair a serious dent in the metal as follows: Slip a thick rubber washer over a ¾-inch wood screw. Turn the screw into the dent's center until the washer is flush with the siding's surface. Using pliers, pull back evenly on the screw head until the metal pops out. Remove the screw; patch the hole with plasticized metal, and refinish the area.
STAINED SIDING	So-called opaque stains react to weather like paint; check them as you would paint. Transparent stains don't peel or deteriorate as paints and opaque stains do, but they fade; when fading starts, it's time to recoat the wood. Examine both types of stained siding once a year for mildew. Scrub off the gray or black blotches with the mix suggested above for painted siding.	Repair a patch of failing opaque stain as you would painted siding. When the time arrives for restaining siding treated with transparent stain, no primer is required. Simply clean the surface and apply new stain. If a transparent stain has faded in blotches, you'll gain a more uniform appearance by applying transparent stain to the entire wall. Scour mildew as soon as it appears.
NATURAL WOOD SIDING	More than one check a year may be necessary for new natural wood siding. Without any finish, redwood, cedar, or cypress siding eventually turns an attractive gray. But during those first years of color transformation, the wood may look blotchy. To hurry the aging process, apply bleaching oils. To slow color-aging, put on a coat of transparent wood preservative. Keep an eye out for mildew, and cure it as noted above for painted siding.	Except for attacking mildew when it shows up, there is little to do on natural wood siding in the nature of touching up. As for larger tasks, if you feel a single application of bleaching oil isn't taking effect fast enough, apply a second coat uniformly. The same approach works for slowing a color change: Apply a second coat of transparent wood preservative.

MAINTAINING FINISHES
(continued)

OTHER SPECIALTY FINISHES

POTENTIAL PROBLEMS

WROUGHT IRON

As tough as wrought iron seems on railings and porch furniture, it's quickly attacked by moisture once bare metal shows through paint. Rusting begins at the spot almost immediately. If left untended, rust could eat through the metal in only a few years. A paint cover protects wrought iron, keeping it as strong as the day it was forged.

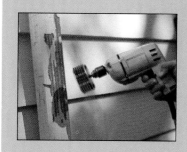

GALVANIZED STEEL

Galvanized steel exposed to weather soon loses its protective zinc coating. Then rust sets in, and because the material is normally used for thin-gauge products such as gutters and downspouts, rust can chew its way through in just a few years. Paint protects the zinc coating.

ALUMINUM

Aluminum doesn't rust, but that doesn't mean it can withstand rain and sun without further treatment. Even anodized aluminum—the kind with a patina on the surface instead of a gloss—deteriorates. Aluminum's equivalent of rust is oxidation, which shows up as a whitish salt. If not removed, oxidation continues until the metal surface is pitted. Pits eventually become holes. Preventive treatments include wax, aluminum paint, and alkyd or latex house paint.

CONCRETE, CONCRETE BLOCK, BRICK

Water readily finds its way into crevices in masonry. Once inside, moisture is on the attack. In winter, a freeze/thaw cycle can turn a tiny masonry crack into a gash. At any time, water weakens masonry by dissolving salts and leaching out binders. A good paint cover or a clear sealer keeps out water and maintains the strength of concrete, concrete block, or brick.

HOW TO MAINTAIN	REFINISHING	SEALANTS/COATINGS
Peeling or flaking paint is the first sign of trouble on wrought iron. Take a wire brush to any spot with loose paint. When you're down to bare metal, finish off the area with emery paper. Smooth the ridge between sound paint and metal. Apply an alkyd primer and either an alkyd or latex finish coat specified for metal.	Assuming wrought iron is maintained well, sand the entire surface with emery paper as preparation for a new coat. The safest course is to apply a new layer of primer (alkyd metal or alkyd zinc chromate) before applying a metal-specified alkyd or latex finish coat.	Although alkyds are solvent-thinned and a little more trouble to use, they are best for the primer and topcoat over wrought iron. If you want a truly tough finish, try an epoxy ester enamel over a primer.
A wire brush and emery paper are the hand-held tools you use to remove loosened paint from galvanized steel. Or use a wire wheel brush attachment on an electric drill to speed the job, as shown *opposite*. Wash the bare metal spot; rinse with vinegar, then water. Wipe dry and apply a primer and topcoat as explained at right.	Rough the surface of sound paint lightly with emery paper and, as with iron, put down either a galvanized metal alkyd or zinc chromate alkyd primer before spraying or brushing on a metal-specified latex or alkyd. Or, if you like, finish with aluminum paint.	There are latex and alkyd primers specifically meant for use on galvanized metal. Finish coats range from low-sheen latex and long-oil alkyds to aluminum paint or tough epoxy ester enamels. Epoxies are an expensive but practical choice to resist air pollution.
You'll find commercial cleaners formulated to remove oxidation from aluminum. Or wash with a mix of strong liquid detergent and warm water. Rinse and wipe dry. Apply car wax if you wish to maintain the metal's color. Otherwise, apply paint as noted at right.	After restoring the clean surface of aluminum, you can keep it that way with auto wax applied every six months or so. To paint aluminum, some experts recommend a primer first (alkyd zinc chromate). Others say that a good finish coat of alkyd, latex, or aluminum paint will survive nearly as well without a primer.	Over clean, bare aluminum, use an alkyd zinc chromate primer for best results, followed by aluminum, alkyd, or latex finish coats. Keep shiny, bare aluminum in that state with liquid car wax, and do nothing but clean anodized aluminum (dull finish).
Sweep away loose debris. Wash the surface with detergent and water and rinse with water. Allow to dry thoroughly. Use a concrete patching product as directed to fill cracks in concrete or concrete block. To smooth a rough concrete surface, parge with a one-part water and one-part mortar mix. Check on the condition of mortar joints and repoint any that are unsound.	Once the surface of masonry is clean and sound, a coat of masonry sealer will protect it for at least a year. Apply with a thick-nap pad, as shown *opposite,* or a roller. Assuming the existing paint is in fair shape, you don't need to apply a primer. Use a masonry-designated latex topcoat for vertical surfaces, a porch-and-floor alkyd for horizontal elements.	Clear masonry sealants, designed to keep out water, should perform through the rainiest of seasons. Water-thinned, easy-to-use latex paints specified for masonry are best for all masonry except concrete patios. There, alkyds stand up better to normal wear and abrasion.

SETTING UP YOUR OWN EXTERIOR MAINTENANCE AGENDA

After reading about all of the exterior maintenance chores discussed in this chapter, you may think you'll be spending every spare minute on a ladder, caulking gun in hand. Actually, unless your house is all but falling down, a conscientious program of preventive maintenance needn't take more than a Saturday or two, twice a year.

Materials don't age at the same rate, or suffer the same exposure to weather. This means that windowsills may require a fresh coat of paint this year, then only a quick scrubbing for the next five. What's more, you needn't attack every problem at once. You might choose in the fall, for example, to simply caulk a piece of split siding as best you can and put replacing it on your list for spring.

The secret to minimizing exterior maintenance jobs is to set up an agenda and stick to it. By systematically inspecting your house and noting things

that must be attended to, you can develop your own plan of attack. A maintenance agenda can be a budgeting tool, too. If, for instance, you know that roofing is deteriorating rapidly, you'll know well in advance that the cost of a new roof is in the offing.

If you live in a warm region, your maintenance schedule can stretch throughout the year, interrupted only by rainy spells. For most of the continental United States, however, most tasks are best done in the spring and fall. Here's a suggested breakdown you can adapt to the situation at your house.

Spring tasks

Once snow, ice, and subfreezing temperatures are past, it's time to see how your home has weathered the winter.
• *Masonry.* Check masonry areas of your home to see how concrete, concrete block, or stone has fared. Mortar joints are the most vulnerable. Look for loose mortar, cracked con-

crete, mildew, and termite tubes. Inspect the foundation, brick or concrete steps, patio, and any brick or stone facing. Look for cracks, signs of settling, and loose mortar joints.
• *Decks and porches.* You'll be using these areas again soon, so look for split boards, flaking paint, and fading stain. Examine railings and posts, benches, and planters for sound construction. Pay special attention to railings people might lean against. How about wrought iron and aluminum railings? They tend to shed paint more rapidly than wood.
• *Eaves, fascias, soffits, and cornices.* Look for mildew, signs of wood rot, and flaking paint. These areas get little sunlight, so they tend to retain moisture, the natural enemy of wood.
• *Gutters and downspouts.* These will need attention in the fall, too, but for now check metal systems for failing paint,

rust, or oxidation; wood systems for rot; and vinyl gutters for warping. Periodically check gutters with a level to see if they tilt evenly toward the downspout opening. Replace worn gutter guards, and install new guards if none exist.

• *Flashing.* Cold weather is toughest on flashings, so spring is the best time to inspect them, preferably before spring rains begin. Follow the suggestions on page 42, and pay special attention to flashing around skylights. While you're inspecting the flashings, take a look at the roofing and correct any flaws you spot.

Fall tasks

Autumn is the time of year when many of us like to put things in order, and that's an especially important aspect of exterior maintenance.

• *Siding.* Summer sun causes many siding failures, especially those related to paint. Fall is the best time to repaint in many regions, so check wood siding carefully. Repair any breaks now, so that winter ice doesn't work its way into the

exterior wall. Tend to other kinds of siding as discussed on page 51.

• *Exterior trim.* Look for flaking paint and incipient wood rot. Check especially sills and drip caps, where water remains longer and sometimes pools.

• *Windows, storm sashes, and shutters.* Replace cracked panes, and remove and apply new glazing compound wherever the old material has dried and cracked. Repair screens before storing them for the winter (ready-made screen patches are available in hardware stores). Check shutters and sashes for loose paint. See that storm sashes fit their openings snugly. If not, install weather stripping.

• *Doors and storm doors.* Examine the paint on doors and trim. See that storm doors fit snugly and that the threshold is sound; this is an area where heat loss is common.

• *Weather stripping and caulking.* From the perspective of saving fuel dollars, these may prove the most vital checks. In many homes, infiltrating air robs more heat than inadequate insulation does. Examine the caulking around every window and door and between all dissimilar materials. Replace torn or crumbling weather stripping .

• *Gutters and downspouts.* Once again, check for rust and deterioration and repair any problems you find. It's especially important to clean out leaves late in the fall. Come winter they could contribute to ice dams that let water back up under roof edges.

• *Chimney.* Examine a masonry chimney for flaws as noted above under masonry. Have the flue cleaned, too, especially if you have a wood-burning stove.

• *Gable and roof vents.* Now is the time to see that no obstruction slows the flow of air. A stuffy attic in winter leads to condensation.

Anytime tasks

Some chores and checkups can be done whenever you have the time and inclination.

• *Roofing and skylights.* Inspection and repairs are easier in good weather. Check joints between the skylight frame and glazing. These may need

a bead of clear caulk. Don't go up on a roof on a hot summer day, though. Many roofing materials, especially those with an asphalt base, soften at high temperatures.

• *Exterior lighting.* Be sure all outdoor fixtures are in good working order; replace burned-out bulbs promptly.

• *Walks and steps.* Eliminate any potential safety hazard right away. Snow, ice, frost-heaving, even wet leaves can cause a bad spill.

• *Garage doors.* To save back strain, attend to a balky garage door right away. Often all that's needed is some lubrication or a minor adjustment. Lubricate electric door openers at the intervals recommended by the manufacturer.

• *Rain, snow, ice, and wind.* After a storm, take a quick stroll around your house. Has wind lifted a shingle or thrown a tree branch against siding? Are gutters icing up? Is water puddling in a spot where it could attack the foundation? Any of these conditions demands prompt action.

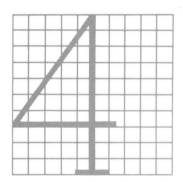

INSIDE YOUR HOME

Maintaining the interior of a home is a continuous process. Dirt and decay, squeaky doors and balky windows, stains on the carpet, and ants in the pantry won't just go away or fix themselves. It takes time, patience, and some do-it-yourself skills to keep a room looking as fresh and clean as the one pictured at right, but perhaps not as much time and patience as you may think. The secret is to keep dirt from building up into grimy layers, and normal wear-and-tear from turning into deterioration. This chapter explains how to handle many common indoor maintenance tasks and helps you organize a method for keeping up with them.

KEEPING CARPET AND UPHOLSTERY LOOKING THEIR BEST

The first rules for keeping your carpet looking fresh and new are: Vacuum frequently—even daily if you have an active family—and wipe up spills and smudges immediately.

About once a year, give your carpeting a thorough cleaning with the type of rental shampooing machine that is best for your carpets and the soil involved.

A *water-extraction machine*, often mistakenly called a "steam cleaner," is best for heavily soiled carpet. The machine forces a chemical solution mixed with hot water (not steam) into the fibers to dissolve and flush out deep-down dirt. Almost simultaneously, it extracts the dirty water with a high-powered vacuum. Stain-removing agents can be used with the machine.

A less-expensive, lighter-weight *wet-shampoo machine* is satisfactory for more lightly soiled carpeting. It scrubs a detergent solution into the nap. When the solution dries, the residue is vacuumed up.

Dry cleaning is the fastest and easiest method. An absorbent powder or granular cleaning compound is brushed into the carpet with a scrubbing brush or by a machine designed for this job. This method won't remove all stains and heavy soil, but it does brighten the carpet and is convenient to use on areas that need frequent cleaning.

This water-extraction carpet shampooer consists of a tank with separate clean and dirty water sections, and a cleaning tool that houses the suction system and vibrating brush. Wheels allow easy maneuvering.

A special dry-cleaning machine with rotating brushes is used to scrub an absorbent granular compound, saturated with detergent and solvent, into the carpet. A vacuum cleaner removes the loosened dirt.

COPING WITH STAINS

Stains usually fall into one of three groups, each requiring a specific cleaning agent. After cleaning, always rinse the area and blot it dry.

• *Water-soluble stains* include alcohol, soft drinks, fruit juices, candy, sugar, and other starches. Sponging with warm water may work. If not, try a solution of a quart of warm water, a tablespoon of mild detergent, and a tablespoon of white vinegar.

• *Oily stains* should be sponged off with a dry-cleaning solvent.

• *Combinations* of water-soluble and oily stains, including peanut butter, crayons, blood, vomit, shoe polish, milk, or coffee, should be cleaned with detergent solution, followed by solvent.

• *Paint.* Detergent solution will remove a recent latex paint stain. Use turpentine on oil-based paint.

• *Candle wax.* Harden the wax with ice cubes wrapped in plastic and scrape off the residue. Draw out the stain with a warm iron pressed over a layer of paper towels.

• *Ink.* Permanent ink stains probably are just that. For other ink stains, use a solvent, then a detergent.

• *Pet urine.* Try a commercial solution designed for pet problems, or a solution of one part vinegar and three parts water.

The same water-extraction machine that cleans your carpet has a separate tool for shampooing deep soil from sofas and chairs. Stroke the tool across the fabric, and the machine injects an upholstery cleaning solution, then sucks up soil and foam. Don't use a carpet-cleaning chemical on upholstery. Be sure to test the fabric for colorfastness by cleaning an inconspicuous area first.

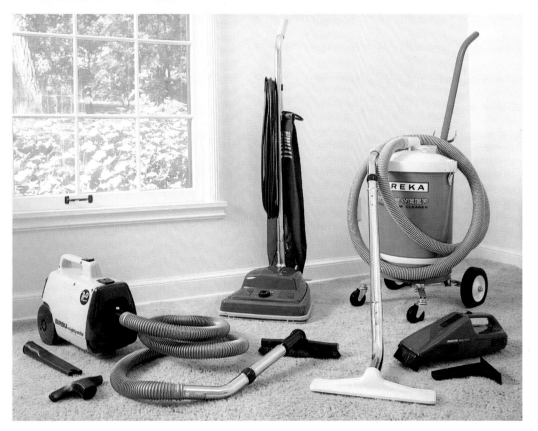

Clockwise from left are four vacuum cleaner options. A canister or tank vacuum, with its straight-suction nozzle, dusts everything, cleans wood, vinyl, and tile floors efficiently, and is best for stairs. The classic upright, with its vibrating brushes and agitator, does best at pulling embedded dirt out of carpets. A heavy-duty shop vacuum sucks up spilled water quickly and cleans up large amounts of debris. A hand-held vacuum can do all sorts of small cleaning chores.

KEEPING WOOD AND TILE FLOORS LOOKING THEIR BEST

Use solvent-based, never water-based, wax for wood floors. You can buff them by hand, but an electric polisher does the job faster and more evenly. Some machines wash and polish.

Vacuum or dry-mop wood floors frequently, and wipe away light soil with a wood cleaner. Lightly wax floors with a regular varnish finish every three months; every six months is enough for a polyurethane finish. Buff between waxings to preserve the gloss.

Water can damage all wood floors, even factory-finished or plastic-coated ones, by seeping through thin spots in the protective finish. This causes black stains that only complete refinishing will remove.

Grease stains also are hard to remove. If steel wool and a solvent don't work, try bleaching them out. Saturate a cotton ball with hydrogen peroxide and place it over the stain. Then saturate a second cotton ball with ammonia and press it over the first, holding it on the stain for three or four minutes. Always rinse off bleaches and spot removers and wipe dry.

White stains, made by spilled alcohol, can be rubbed away with fine steel wool and mineral oil. Try the same treatment for *urine stains.* If this doesn't work, soak the spot with vinegar.

Rub *chewing gum, crayon marks, candle wax,* or *tar* with ice cubes (in a plastic bag) until the residue is brittle and can be scraped off. Loosen any remaining marks with a little cleaning fluid poured around the edges.

Rub away *mildew stains* with a mild solution of trisodium phosphate and chlorine bleach.

Erase surface stains and shallow scratches with steel wool and a cleaning solvent. Then rub the area with wax; if necessary, renew the finish, feathering it onto the surrounding area.

RESTORING WOOD FLOORS

First repair damaged boards, set protruding nailheads, and fill the holes. Then, sand off the old finish, apply stain or filler, and apply one of these finishes:
• *Polyurethane* or other clear plastic. By far the most durable choice.
• *Regular varnish.* Less costly, but not as long-wearing in traffic areas.
• *Penetrating sealer.* Gives a low-gloss, easy-to-touch-up finish.

Ceramic floor tiles are exceptionally durable. Unglazed types develop a patina, so they often are easier to maintain as they age. All tiles have to be cleaned regularly though. If they're not too grimy, wash them with a sponge mop and a commercial tile cleaner or an all-purpose household detergent.

For *beverage, dye,* and *fruit stains,* you may need a chlorine bleach solution (three tablespoons of bleach to a quart of water). Keep the area wet until the stain fades.

Wash away *mildew stains* with a mildew stain remover or with chlorine bleach and trisodium phosphate in water. Spray floors regularly with a mildew germicide.

Some unglazed tiles are very porous and should be coated with a stain-resistant sealer, especially if they're in a kitchen or bathroom. Some sealers leave the tile looking natural, without a shine; others give a high gloss that's even shinier if you wax it.

Grout, the material between the tiles, is susceptible to staining and mildew. Using a toothbrush, scrub on an all-purpose product that cleans, disinfects, and kills mildew. If this doesn't remove all the stain, rub on a paste of scouring powder and water, leave it on for five hours, and then rinse and dry. Apply an acrylic joint sealer to the clean grout, even if you don't seal the tiles.

Protect unglazed tiles with a silicone sealer. Spread the sealer on small areas with a scrub brush and on large areas with a buffing machine. Apply two or more thin coats. Polish each coat, while it's wet, with the machine. When the sealer begins to dry (you'll feel a pull on the brush), put a clean pad on the machine and buff the floor to a mirror finish.

MAINTAINING WOODWORK

Woodwork—ceiling moldings and baseboards, sills, frames, and panels—needs regular dusting. Occasionally you may need to revitalize it with fresh paint or varnish.

Because woodwork is composed of many dust-catching surfaces, it should be dusted weekly. A lamb's wool duster with a telescoping handle is the best tool for whisking dirt from high and hard-to-reach places.

For best results on *varnished surfaces,* apply a dust-attracting spray to the duster. Clean varnish and other clear finishes with a special-purpose commercial cleaner-polish.

Lightly wash soiled *painted woodwork* with a mild solution of trisodium phosphate. For *glossy enamels,* which may be dulled by a strong cleaner, use a gentle oil soap dissolved in water. You may need a heavy-duty foam cleaner if painted woodwork is extra-dirty.

Painting and varnishing

If your woodwork looks shabby even when it's just been cleaned, you may need to give it a fresh finish.

First, give the surface a thorough washing, rinsing, and sanding. If the paint is flaking, if there are several layers, or if you plan to varnish formerly painted surfaces, you'll need to strip the woodwork.

To do this, apply a paste stripper, which will stick to vertical surfaces. Leave it on for 15 minutes, then scrape off the old finish. Sand after every step and dust immediately. Pick up the fine dust and residue with a tack cloth, a barely damp cotton cloth impregnated with a little turpentine and varnish. Then neutralize the surface, following directions on the container.

Fill dents, scratches, and other imperfections with wood filler. Use a primer on new or freshly stripped woodwork before painting.

If you are varnishing rather than painting, consider using a sealer even if the directions on the varnish container don't suggest it. A sealer promotes even absorption of varnish on softwood veneers and keeps recently applied stain from bleeding.

Apply two or more coats of varnish, letting each cure for 24 hours. Finish with a good carnauba paste wax. Buff with a soft cloth for a high gloss.

Brush on varnish with the grain and feather-brush where strokes overlap. Shallow marks will disappear as varnish dries.

PAINT AND VARNISH OPTIONS

• *Polyurethane varnish* is the longest-lasting, has the hardest surface, and provides the most transparent finish.
• *Epoxy* and other high-gloss *plastics* are mar-resistant.
• *Alkyd-based varnishes* are less costly than polyurethane and resist scuffing well.
• *Water-based synthetic varnish* makes cleanup easier but is not as durable as alkyd-based varnishes.
• *Polyurethane paints* are pigmented versions of clear polyurethane varnish.
• *Solvent-thinned paints,* usually alkyd-based, require a solvent for cleanup, but generally are more durable than latex and less expensive than polyurethane.
• *Water-thinned paints,* such as latex, are easy to clean up.

MAINTAINING WALL COVERINGS

Most synthetic wall paneling can be scrubbed with a strong household detergent solution, but test any cleaning product on an inconspicuous spot before applying it to large areas. Always rinse thoroughly and buff dry.

Paper and vinyl wall coverings are generally labeled "scrubbable," "washable," or "nonwashable." *Scrubbable* wall coverings, made of vinyl or vinyl-impregnated paper, can, if necessary, be scrubbed with a heavy-duty or foam cleanser. *Washable* papers have thin coatings of vinyl acetate and can be sponged with a mild detergent solution. *Nonwashable* papers must be dry-cleaned. Dust all types frequently.

To clean *washable wall coverings*, use a well-wrung-out sponge for both washing and rinsing. Clean *nonwashable papers* with a commercial wall cleaner or give them a gentle rubdown with a specially treated terry cloth towel wrapped around a dust mop. First, soak the towel in turpentine, wring it out, and air-dry it thoroughly, then wipe the walls from ceiling to floor, replacing the soiled towel as necessary.

Special wall coverings
Some *flocked wallpaper* can be washed, but check the label. After cleaning flocked paper, brush it gently to bring up the nap. *Metal foil laminates* are as sturdy as vinyl and can be scrubbed. Some *foil papers,* however, merely have a thin metallic coating and may not be washable. *Fabrics laminated to paper backings* may have vinyl coatings and can be sponged clean. Those without plastic coatings are almost impossible to clean if they are badly soiled.

Gently wipe soiled *silk, grass cloth, burlap,* and *yarn* with a sponge dampened in a mild detergent solution. Clean *felt* with a granular rug cleaner; water may shrink it or change the color.

OTHER WALL COVERINGS

• *Ceramic tiles.* Glazed tiles scratch easily and should be protected from sharp objects. Wipe off soil with sudsy water. Grease stains are hard to remove from unglazed tiles. Try a heavy-duty cleaner, scrubbing it on with a scrub brush. Seal cleaned tiles to keep them stain-free.
• *Barn boards.* If barn-board paneling was not thoroughly cleaned prior to installation, scrub it with a stiff-bristle brush and heavy-duty cleanser in hot water to which you've added household disinfectant. Rub on linseed oil, but don't stain the boards or you will lose their silver-gray color. Seal the boards if they're in a bathroom or kitchen.
• *Cork.* Vacuum it regularly, wash it with a mild detergent, and rinse.
• *Mirror panels* and *tiles.* Clean with a commercial glass cleaner; tap water will leave streaks. Don't spray cleaner on glass; instead, moisten a cloth with it. Wipe up any drips quickly. If moisture seeps into the back of the mirror, it can cause the silvering to separate from the glass. Give the cleaned mirror a gleam by polishing it with rubbing alcohol.
• *Brick veneer.* These flat tilelike bricks are easy to wash if you seal them with a nonglossy sealer. Scrub away grease stains on unsealed bricks with a half-cup of TSP in two gallons of water. If the stain persists, apply a thick paste of powdered whiting and benzine. Hold the poultice in place for an hour with plastic wrap taped to the wall.

When cleaning washable wall coverings, use only as much moisture as necessary. Dip a sponge in cleaning solution, wring well, and wipe the wall. Rinse and then go over the surface with a barely damp sponge to wipe away streaks.

Paneling

Dust all types of paneling regularly, and wipe away light soil with a special-purpose cleaner-polish that hides surface scratches and scuff marks. Read all packaging instructions carefully: Some polishes, for wood only, contain solvents that will etch nonwood paneling surfaces.

For wood paneling that has been neglected, you will need a stronger solvent, such as a paint thinner. Do a small area at a time and wipe away solvent and loosened dirt before the solvent dries.

Rub stubborn spots with a little mineral oil and pumice, being careful not to rub through the finish. Restore the shine by waxing and buffing.

If the wood is very cloudy or if blemishes extend through the finish, you may have to strip and refinish the panel.

Repair scratches with a filler stick made for covering nail holes, and touch up with stain.

Factory-finished synthetic paneling, in large sheets or planks, has a baked-in finish that enables you to wipe light soil away easily. Use a heavy-duty cleaner to remove heavier soil. Scrub away mildew with a solution of one cup of trisodium phosphate (TSP), one quart of chlorine bleach, and three quarts of warm water. The TSP will remove grime and wet the surface so bleach can work and kill the fungus. As a preventive, spray all paneling in any damp area periodically with a mildew germicide.

Note that both vinyl-covered and solid wood paneling should be waxed when first installed, and then cleaned and rewaxed every few years.

To remove stains on textured paper, moisten a rag with dry-cleaning fluid and dab lightly at the spot. Rubbing can remove part of the textured surface.

Flocked papers and fabrics such as grass cloth and silk may be damaged if you dust them with a cloth. Use the soft brush attachment of your vacuum cleaner.

USING MOPS
AND BROOMS

SWEEPING AND MOPPING OPTIONS

TYPE	CARE

BROOMS

A good-quality corn broom is made of a mixture of curly and rough fibers stitched to-gether. Some nylon brooms have special magnetic bristles with split tips that pick up more of the fine dirt. Others have wide-flared bristles for big spaces.

To clean a broom, swish it in hot soapy water, rinse, and hang to dry. Restore the broom's shape by wrapping rubber bands around the wet bristles. Always hang a broom or stand it on end, never on the bristles.

DRY MOPS

Dry mops, or dust mops, pick up more than brooms and are better for cleaning up tracked-in grit. But they don't sweep out corners and edges of flooring as well as brooms do.

Don't bang a dry mop against a windowsill or door jamb to shake off the dust. If you can, take it outside to shake it; if that's not possible, shake it into a paper bag or vacuum it. If the mop head comes off the frame, periodically wash it in the washing machine. To wash a gummy mop, add a half-cup of ammonia to the wash cycle. Swish an attached mop up and down in sudsy water. Rinse, shake to fluff up the yarn, and let air-dry.

SPONGE MOPS

A sponge mop is a good mul-tipurpose cleaning tool, handy for wiping down walls as well as mopping floors.

Soak sponge mops before use; they are brittle when dry. Strong cleaning solutions and bleaches will damage them. Rinse well after every use and dry away from heat.

WET MOPS

A high-quality wet mop has long strings of sturdy yarn that soak up water. The mop head may be attached to the handle or may fit a clamp-type handle.

Mops used with cleaning compounds need thorough rinsing after every use. Squeeze out the water and hang the mop to dry. Snip off frayed ends. Never store a mop wet in a pail or with the mop head on the floor, or the yarn will mildew and develop an offensive odor.

Soft, synthetic bristles are better than harsh corn brooms for no-wax vinyl floors. Corn brooms are better for all other surfaces. An angled broom does a good job in corners and under kitchen cabinets. Use an outdoor broom in basements.

Use a dry mop on any type of hard or resilient flooring. A double-action mop head that swivels is good for cleaning under beds and other hard-to-reach spots. Don't put floor polish or oil on a dust mop that you plan to use on waxed floors.

A good sponge mop is ideal for washing and rinsing all types of flooring. Do not use one on rough surfaces.

These are standby cleaning tools, used for mopping every type of flooring, even rough stone and cement. They're especially useful for cleaning large areas.

DON'T FORGET ABOUT THESE

Maintaining the big expanses in a home—its walls and floors, woodwork, and doors—is important. Neglecting smaller areas, however, may spoil the whole effect. Look around your house for spots likely to be neglected. Here are some areas that it's easy to overlook.

Chandeliers and ceiling fixtures

A crystal chandelier is a thing of beauty only if its faceted pendants are sparkling. For routine care, spray on a nonabrasive cleaner, especially made for fine crystals. The cleaner drips off, taking dirt with it.

If a chandelier is coated with greasy dirt, you may have to disassemble it and wash the parts in warm water and a mild detergent. Rinse them, then polish with a soft cloth. If the wire pins or hooks that link prisms to the fixture are rusted or disintegrated, replace them.

Clean brass or copper ceiling fixtures with soapy water, and rub on a good commercial metal polish to remove tarnish. Avoid steel wool and abrasives.

Fireplace

If a fireplace is used frequently, the chimney should be cleaned annually to prevent an accumulation of flammable creosote on chimney walls. (More about this on page 49.)

Soot stains on brickwork often can be removed by scrubbing them with a fiber brush (not a wire brush). Use only clear water. Remove stubborn stains with a mild solution of muriatic acid and water.

If a detergent solution doesn't remove soot stains from a marble mantel, wash the area with hydrogen peroxide mixed with a few drops of ammonia. Deep stains sometimes can be lifted out with a poultice of powdered whiting and chlorine laundry bleach. After cleaning, polish the marble with pumice and rottenstone.

Radiators

Vacuum behind and underneath radiators with the wand attachment of your cleaner, or dust them with a special radiator brush. Use the same brush, dipped in suds, to wash these areas.

Roller window shades

Dust window shades frequently to keep them looking fresh. Many good-quality shades are treated so they can be wiped clean with a damp cloth.

Eventually, a shade will need a more thorough cleaning. Place it on a flat surface and wash it section by section with a sudsy cloth or sponge and as little water as possible. Damp-rinse each section before going on to the next. Turn the shade over and repeat the process on the other side.

Hang the shade at the window and pull it down to full length. Let it dry for 24 hours. Roll the dry shade to the top, leave it this way for several hours, and the shade will have a crisp, ironed look.

Nonwashable shades can be refreshed with wallpaper cleaner, although some textured styles may need professional dry cleaning.

Miniblinds and venetian blinds

Aluminum miniblinds are a breeze to maintain. Simply dust them with a vacuum attachment or soft cloth, and wash with a mild cleanser occasionally.

Dust is more likely to cling to wooden venetian blinds. Use a dusting mitt or a special venetian blind tool with fingers that slide between the slats.

Wash lightly soiled painted blinds with a mild detergent; use spray-on foam cleaner for heavy soil.

Clean wood-tone blinds with a good wood cleaner-polish.

Interior shutters

Clean louvered shutters as you would venetian blinds. Use a creamy liquid wax for wood grains, and spray-on foam cleaner for painted wood.

ORGANIZING A CLEANING CLOSET

Compartments help organize the cleaning closet illustrated opposite, with shelves, a rolling bin, and a locked child-proof cabinet. A wire rack on the door helps control clutter. In the kitchen shown below, a prebuilt cabinet holds cleaning supplies. Bifold doors close to conceal laundry equipment and supplies.

Well-organized storage for cleaning implements and supplies saves time and energy in the never-ending process of maintaining your home.

Locate a cleaning closet as close to points of use as possible. A utility room, kitchen, or hallway is a logical downstairs location. You may want to store some duplicate equipment and cleansers on an upper floor.

If you don't have an existing closet that can be adapted, you can build one. A space about 24 inches wide, 20 inches deep, and 65 inches high is adequate. Many prefabricated freestanding cabinets also can be tailored to fit your needs.

Gather your cleaning equipment and measure items before finishing the interior.

Provide little "garages" for the vacuum cleaner, floor scrubber, and other large equipment, with space for hoses and attachments. An upright vacuum cleaner needs a niche about 48 inches high. A canister vacuum may take twice as much floor space, but not as much headroom.

Bracket shelving, hung on metal strips, can be adjusted as needs change. Be sure to include an area that can be locked for storing chemicals and caustic cleaning aids. Use every inch of space. Line walls with pegboard to hold brackets and hooks for hanging brooms, dustpans, and mops.

The inside of a closet door can provide bonus storage. Install pegboard, a vinyl-coated metal rack, or a series of small shelves, like those on a refrigerator door, with guardrails to keep items from falling off.

Hinged doors on closets give quick access to what's inside, but if clearance is limited, consider using sliding or bifold doors.

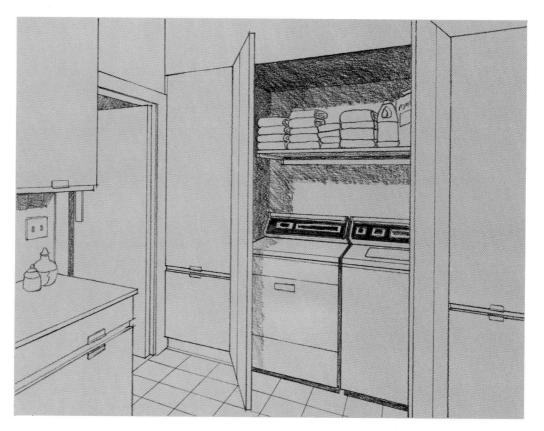

STOCKING A CLEANING CLOSET

Products used for regular cleaning and maintenance fall into the general categories listed here. Buy other products as needed.
• *Abrasives,* such as household scouring powders, clean by scraping dirt loose.
• *Absorbents,* such as fuller's earth, cornmeal, and baking soda, absorb oil, grease, and moisture.
• *Bleaches* include strong chlorine laundry bleaches, milder powder oxygen bleaches, and such products as lemon juice, vinegar, ammonia, hydrogen peroxide, and muriatic acid.
• *Boosters,* such as washing soda, borax, and trisodium

phosphate, make detergents more effective.
• *Caustic products* include cleaners for drains, toilet bowls, and ovens.
• *Detergents* are synthetic cleaners that work in hot or cold water or in hard water.
• *Disinfectants* kill bacteria, mold, mildew, and odors.
• *Dry-cleaning fluids* are commercial water-free solvents that lift and dissolve dirt.
• *Lubricants* include oils, glycerin, petroleum jelly, powdered graphite, and silicone sprays. Use them to reduce friction or soften stains.
• *Soaps,* made from animal

or vegetable fats, usually do not work well in cold or hard water.
• *Specialized products* range from bathroom tile-and-tub cleaners, window cleaners, and chandelier spray rinses to powders and foam shampoos for carpets and upholstery. Dozens of waxes, oils, polishes, and cleaners are available for wood or resilient floors and for furniture.

Also keep on hand any necessary pesticides, a little rubbing alcohol to give glass a gleam, acetone for removing paint stains, and a bottle of club soda for quick treatment of stains in fabrics.

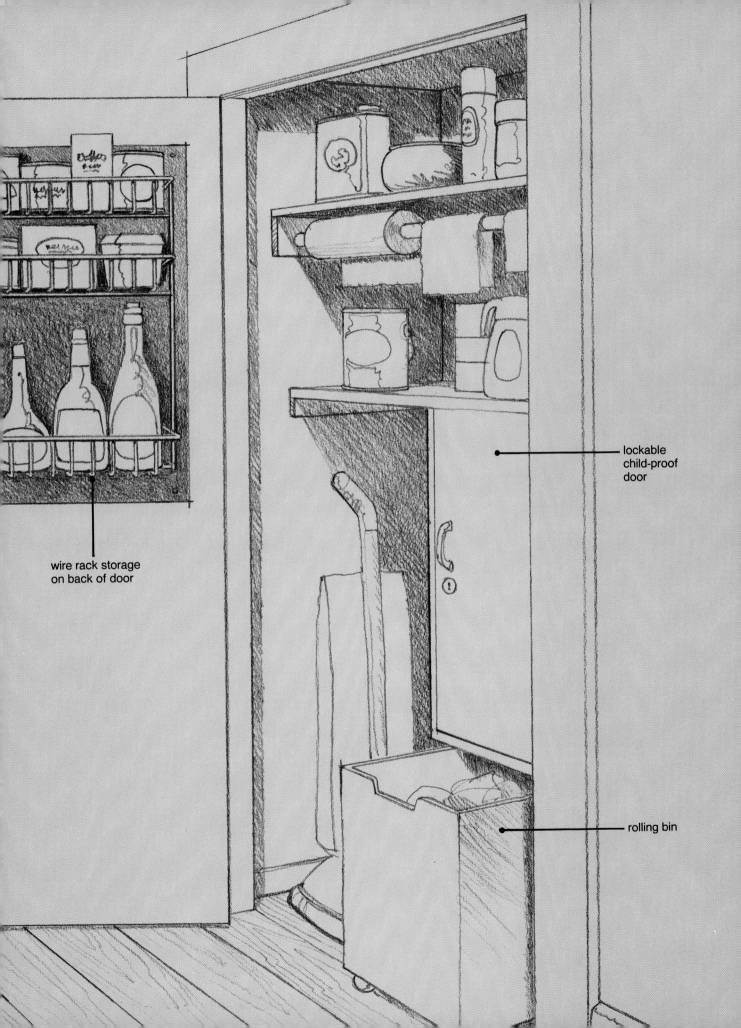

wire rack storage
on back of door

lockable
child-proof
door

rolling bin

KEEPING DOORS MOVING SMOOTHLY

Doors that rattle or stick or won't shut are irritating problems. A little adjusting, tightening, or lubricating of hardware may solve the problem.

To fix a binding door, first check its hinges. Screws holding the hinge plate to the door or frame may be loose. Replace them with longer screws, or plug screw holes with wood dowels and drill holes for new screws.

A sticking door also may be tilted in its frame because of sagging hinges. If the binding occurs at the bottom or on the latch side, the top hinge probably is at fault. Deepen its mortise and reset the top hinge.

You may need to shim out the bottom hinge by building it up with a thin piece of particleboard under the hinge plate. If the bottom hinge sags, deepen its mortise and reset the hinge, or shim out the top hinge.

A rattling door that won't latch securely may have a strike plate out of line. File a hole in the plate to enlarge the opening, so the latch can seat. If there's a big disparity, relocate the strike plate.

If the strike is too far away to engage the latch, shim it out with thin pieces of wood under the strike or by using two strike plates, one on top of the other. You may have to shim hinges as well.

Locks

If the lock sticks, it usually means grease applied at the factory has become dirty and gummy. Remove doorknobs and unscrew and lift out the lock body. Wash it in a petroleum solvent and apply penetrating oil to the moving parts.

This is the only time oil should be used on a lock. Use graphite for regular lubrication, as explained at right.

The best way to lubricate a keyway is with powdered graphite, sold in tubes at hardware stores. Puff a tiny amount of graphite into the **keyhole—don't oil or grease a keyway, or the tumblers won't be able to exert enough friction to work the latch bolt.**

PROTECT WALLS FROM WAYWARD DOORS

If doors bang back and gouge holes in walls, or slam and flap in the breeze, consider installing some devices that will keep them in their places.

• *Doorstops.* These come in several forms. You can attach hinge-pin stops to one of the door hinges, or screw a spindle with a padded tip to the back of the door or into the baseboard behind the door. If you have pets or children, the hinge pin stop is safer; the projecting type can inflict a painful bruise on an animal or crawling child.

• *Bumpers.* Decorative bumpers attach behind the door and hold it open.
• *Closures.* These are spring units with pneumatic tubes; they close doors automatically.
• *Protective plates.* Kick plates and push plates of plastic, metal, or ceramic, will shield parts of doors that are vulnerable to kicks and scratches. A large escutcheon will keep the keyhole area unmarred. Protective plates are available in a range of styles and can be decorative as well as functional.

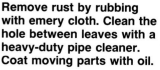

A little machine oil may quiet squeaky hinges, but rusty hinges need cleaning and lubricating. Dismantle and clean one pin at a time. **Remove rust by rubbing with emery cloth. Clean the hole between leaves with a heavy-duty pipe cleaner. Coat moving parts with oil.**

Pocket doors rarely malfunction. Like most sliding doors, they glide on self-lubricating wheels and need no oiling. If a door is out of line, turn the cog screw at the top to level it. Check with a bubble level held along the leading edge.

If bypass doors do not slide smoothly, check the roller mechanism. The plates can slip out of alignment. If that's the case, realign them and tighten the screws. Adjust the dial on the hardware to raise or lower the door so it will ride properly.

To adjust sliding doors, tighten any loose adjusting screws on the glide and on hardware that holds the doors in line. To adjust the height, turn the screw at the bottom of the jamb. Keep tracks clean, and lubricate them with graphite or candle wax.

If folding or bifold doors stick, adjust the hardware near the floor and on the header. Use a wrench to twist the screw, or lower the pivot bracket to raise or lower the doors and get them plumb.

MAINTAINING
WINDOWS

Maintaining windows doesn't end with keeping the glass gleaming. Windows must be kept functioning, too.

The most common problem is a sash that opens or closes reluctantly. Check for loose screws, bent metal, swollen wood, rust, and caked dirt. Clean and lubricate channels and mechanisms on all windows twice a year.

Straighten slightly bent or swollen tracks, jambs, or stops by placing a block of wood at the sticking point and tapping it with a hammer.

To release a paint-stuck double-hung window, force a broad-blade putty knife between the sash and the stop, working the blade back and forth. If this doesn't break the paint seal, try prying the sash up from the outside.

If a window won't stay open, or jams in the track, the mechanism probably is at fault. To replace a broken sash cord in an older double-hung window, remove the sash and the access plate that covers sash weights inside the jamb. Thread a new cord over the pulley and tie it to the sash and weight.

Spring-loaded sash balances, used in newer construction, cannot be repaired. If one is broken, replace it.

The sashes in these double-hung windows will slide up and down smoothly only if channels are clear and smooth. Clean wood or metal channels with a chisel, using a steady pressure to pare away gummy dirt and dried paint. Clean plastic channels with steel wool. Lubricate channels by rubbing with a block of paraffin or candle wax, or use a silicone spray lubricant.

Deteriorated glazing compound should be replaced. First, scrape away all cracked or dried-out compound with a putty knife, screwdriver, or old chisel. With a wood window, brush linseed oil into the channel. Roll the compound into a rope and press it into the channel. Finally, bevel the new compound by drawing a putty knife along it. Let the compound dry for a week before painting. For more about glazing, see page 45.

When a combination screen and storm window balks, check for oxidation in its tracks. If you find corrosion, clean with a detergent solution. Scrub away stubborn stains with fine steel wool and naval jelly, then lubricate with candle wax or silicone spray. Check caulking around frames periodically.

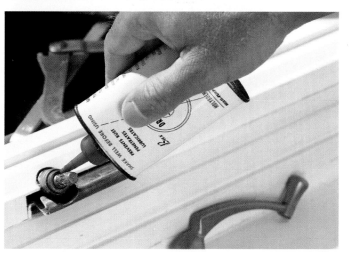

To lubricate a casement window, remove the crank handle of the operating mechanism and apply a few drops of household oil or silicone lubricant. If grease is encrusted inside the operator, dismantle the unit, wash it with kerosene, dry it, then coat the gears with petroleum jelly or graphite. Scrape debris out of the extension arm track with a wire brush and spray with silicone. Lubricate hinges and latch pivots, too.

CONTROLLING
PESTS

PESTS AND WHAT TO DO ABOUT THEM

PEST	HABITAT	HOW TO ELIMINATE THEM
ANTS	Most small ants are in the kitchen. Big carpenter ants nest in rotting wood.	Spray entry points with an ant-and-roach insecticide, and use sweetened poison bait. Destroy nests of carpenter ants with foam or powdered pesticide or call in an exterminator.
CARPET BEETLES	They may be in the carpet, even though you don't see them.	Spray carpeting and furniture and along edges of baseboards periodically with a water-emulsion, residual pesticide.
COCK-ROACHES	They come in with the groceries, up through drains and steam pipes, or through gaps in walls.	Discourage them with meticulous housekeeping. Keep food in sealed containers. Kill them with repeated applications of special ant-and-roach poisons.
CRICKETS	They swarm into the house in late summer and chew holes in fabrics.	Create a barrier of residual pesticide along doorways and other entry points. Spray insecticide where you hear crickets.
FLEAS	These prefer your pets, but they will attack you, too, and can infest your home.	Use flea powders and sprays recommended by your veterinarian for your pet. Spray infested premises, and use an indoor fogger for serious infestation or call in an exterminator.
MOSQUI-TOES	They breed in stagnant water.	Clean out breeding spots in your yard; community action may be needed to eliminate other breeding places and for fogging large areas. Screen your windows and kill mosquitoes with a swatter or space spray as necessary.
MOTHS	You'll find the larvae happily eating away on stored woolens.	Seal woolen garments in bags with moth crystals. Spray closets with a mothproofing product.
PANTRY PESTS	"Bran bugs" or "flour beetles" often infest cereals, flour, or grains.	Keep shelves wiped clean and store food in tight containers. Coat shelves with a liquid pesticide. Don't put food back until shelves are dry.
RATS AND MICE	Some live indoors year-round; others come in during cold weather.	Kill with traps and poison bait. Seal entry holes and see that food is not left out to attract rodents.
SQUIRRELS, BATS, AND RACCOONS	They may set up homes in attics or chimneys.	Smoke them out of a chimney. Sprinkle moth crystals on an attic floor to drive them out, then seal all potential entrances with mortar, sheet metal, or hardware cloth.

No home is free of pests. You can, however, control them with good sanitation in areas where they shelter and feed, and by the proper use of chemicals.

Don't treat pesticides casually. Although you can buy them at your supermarket, they are poisons. Most over-the-counter sprays and dusts are safe for home use, if you buy a product recommended for *indoor* use and apply it precisely according to directions.

Read the label carefully before you buy. Not all insecticides kill all types of insects. Most *ant-and-roach insecticides* are effective against a broad range of crawling insects, but should not be sprayed into the air. They have a potent, residual action. *Flying insect pesticides,* designed for space spraying, usually kill crawling bugs, too, but only on contact. They are not effective for treating areas where insects travel.

Safety precautions
- Always store pesticides in locked cabinets and in their original containers.
- Most sprays, fogs, and concentrates are flammable. Lighted cigarettes, open flames, and even pilot lights can ignite them.
- Keep children and pets away from any area that is being treated until the surfaces are dry. Place toxic baits and poisoned dust where they will not be accessible to children and animals.
- Do not spray over food, dishes, or cooking utensils.
- Wash your hands after handling any chemical. If it spills on your skin, wash it off immediately. If it is swallowed or gets in eyes, follow the first aid treatment listed on the label and get prompt medical treatment.

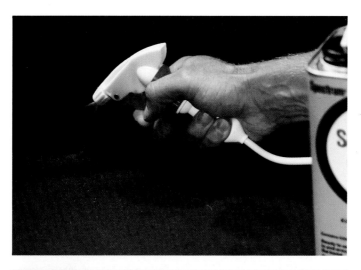

Moths, carpet beetles, fleas, and other insects may invade upholstered furniture. Spray under cushions and in pleats, crevices, folds, and corners. Use a surface insecticide labeled for use on fabrics; some oil-based formulas will stain carpets and upholstery. Even a water-based concentrate may spot fabrics and wood, so test it first.

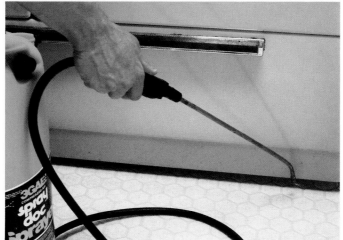

For hard-to-reach crevices between counters, in tight corners, and behind appliances, use a compressed-air sprayer with an adjustable wand that dispenses liquid or foam insecticide and forces it into the crannies. The insecticide will dry on the surface and remain effective for weeks. As insects run over treated areas, the poison, absorbed by their bodies, will kill them.

Cracks and small openings provide good spots for crawling insects to enter and escape, to hide and multiply. Caulk cracks around bathtubs, countertops, and sinks, especially those behind backsplashes. Fill gaps in floorboards, walls, and baseboards with wood putty. Push wads of steel wool into wider spaces around water pipes and conduits. Then fill with a sealant.

SETTING UP YOUR OWN INSIDE MAINTENANCE AGENDA

Whole-house cleaning used to be a springtime ritual, scheduled for about the time the lilacs began to bud. The house was stripped and torn up for days, meals were haphazard, and the smell of soap and furniture polish filled the air.

Now cleaning and maintenance can be less disruptive. Much of it should go on quietly all year long. Modern floors have mar-proof finishes, and carpets and upholstery repel stains. An array of laborsaving equipment and cleaning products makes the work easier.

Your particular maintenance agenda depends on many things—the size and age of your home, the number of family members and pets, the types of furnishings, and the kind and amount of entertaining you do.

It's essential to have a maintenance schedule—one that is strict enough to work, yet flexible enough to let you do most of the chores at your own pace and at convenient times.

The following agenda is based on the premise that preventive maintenance is the best kind. It is cheaper and more efficient to clean and repair things regularly or when they need it, than it is to let everything go for one big binge in the spring or fall.

Regular inspection
Make an inspection tour of the interior of your home every three months. Examine all areas carefully, room by room and floor by floor.
• *Check for safety hazards.* Is your fireplace damper working properly? Are sash cords so loose that a window could crash down on someone's hand? Be on the alert for dangers such as poisonous chemicals left about casually, frayed electrical cords, unscreened fireplaces, and loose carpeting on stairs—anything that could harm family or visitors. Inspect locks to be sure your home is not an easy target for burglars.
• *Check for energy leaks.* Is weather stripping or caulking around doors and windows in good repair? Are there gaps around exposed electrical joints and outlets? Is the fireplace damper always closed when the fireplace is not in use?
• *Check for damage or potential damage.* Look for flaking paint, mildew, swollen wood, or signs of decay on walls, ceilings, and woodwork and around all openings. Find the source of the dampness that is causing these problems. Poke around in dark cupboards for signs of insects or mice, and for cracks, damp areas, or spilled foods that might attract them. Once you've identified problem areas, clean or repair them as soon as possible.

Cleaning schedule
You may prefer to clean the whole house once a week, or find it easier to sandwich the thorough cleaning of one room into each day's schedule. The following schedule suggests things that need doing on a daily, weekly, or long-term basis. Adapt the ideas to suit your way of life.
• *Daily.* As much as possible, keep dirt from coming in by using mats at entrance doorways and a shoe scraper on the porch.

Clear up clutter as you go, and wipe up spills when they happen.

Encourage family members to pick up, hang up, put away, and clean up after themselves. Everyone should wash up snack dishes, wipe the bathroom sink after every use, and clean the shower or tub so it's ready for the next person.

Load the dishwasher as soon as possible after every meal, or put the dishes in the sink to soak until you have time to wash them.

Before you go to bed at night, empty ashtrays, replace books, magazines, or any clutter.

There are plenty of other daily chores—making beds, dusting tabletops, and running a carpet sweeper over traffic lanes to clean up tracked-in dirt—but they can be done more smoothly if the house is tidy.

• *Weekly.* Do cleaning your own way, but do it regularly. You may prefer to strip and re-make all the beds, then go back and clean the rooms. Or you may find it easier to do each room completely before going on to the next.

Your schedule should include dusting and vacuuming of walls and woodwork, so dirt won't mix with moisture and smoke in the air and settle in as impregnated soil. Wipe door jambs with a detergent solution, dust windowsills and panes, and wash off finger marks with a spray cleaner.

Dust wood furniture, and every few weeks vacuum upholstered pieces. Get into corners and back of and under furniture with vacuum attachments; about once a month move furniture out for a good cleaning of areas behind it.

While you are vacuuming the floor, clean up any spots or stains you may see.

Try to clean one out-of-sight area—a closet, storage room, or drawer—once a month.

Use a good disinfectant foam cleaner in the bathroom, on sink, tub or shower, toilet tank and lid, and any exposed pipes.

A kitchen alone can take the better part of a day to clean if you let things go, or if you have a large family to feed. Try to clean one large appliance, such as the refrigerator or the stove, or one large area, such as storage cabinets, once a month.

Once in a while

Some cleaning and maintenance tasks may need doing twice a year, some only every two or three years.

Once a year, move all the furniture out of each room, if possible, and clean from ceiling to floor. Dust or vacuum everything, including light bulbs, air conditioning outlets, and heat vents.

Walls and ceilings may not need an overall washing every year, but clean areas along stairways, which get heavy use. Repaint or repaper, if necessary.

Wash woodwork yearly and retouch chipped paint if you are not redecorating.

If wall paneling looks dull, clean off old wax and dirt and rewax.

Wash windowpanes, inside and out, twice a year. Polish the picture window and the glass in doors on the front of the house more frequently—these are areas everyone notices. Don't forget to vacuum

and wash screens and window shades. Lubricate, repair, or replace moving parts on windows and doors, if necessary.

Shampoo carpeting, clean and rewax hard- and resilient-surface floors.

Clean, wax, or polish all wooden furniture and refinish or repair damaged wood.

Vacuum all upholstered furniture, including mattresses, thoroughly; turn mattresses twice a year, alternating end-to-end and side-to-side. Air bedding and fluff pillows in your dryer.

Send soiled draperies to be cleaned. If they're not soiled, brush them well and hang them on a line outdoors for a few hours.

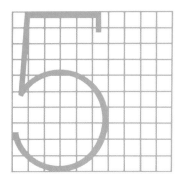

KITCHENS AND BATHS

Kitchens and baths are homes to pipes and fixtures, and where water runs, plumbing maintenance follows. There's more to kitchens and baths than plumbing, though. They also present special cleaning problems, and typically have a multitude of cabinet doors and drawers that can malfunction. This chapter explains how to handle minor plumbing emergencies, how to keep drawers and cabinets operating smoothly, and how to keep surfaces sparkling.

MAINTAINING DOORS AND DRAWERS

Opening and closing doors and drawers should be a process you hardly notice. When a door fails to stay shut or a drawer balks at sliding in and out, a few simple procedures can get it on the right track.

Drawers slide on glides, which may be along the sides of the drawer or at the center of the drawer's bottom. To prevent sticking, spray silicone lubricants on the runners or edges of the drawer. Rubbing hard wax or soap on the glides also can keep drawers working smoothly. If these remedies fail, examine the glides for damage; replace badly worn or bent glides.

Sometimes the drawer itself is at fault. If a side or bottom has worked loose, tighten it by disassembling the drawer, cleaning old glue off the parts, then reassembling. Reinforce corners with corner blocks or molding.

Humidity can cause a drawer to swell. On a dry day when the drawer is moving smoothly, shellac or varnish the drawer sides inside and out to help keep them from absorbing moisture in damp weather.

Most cabinet doors have some type of two-piece metal catch that keeps the door shut—one part is installed on the door, the other on the edge of the frame. The screws holding the catches can work loose, throwing the two parts out of alignment.

Sometimes built-up paint is the culprit. Ball or roller catches will malfunction if paint prevents their parts from moving freely. Remove the hardware, soak in paint thinner to clean, then reinstall and spray with silicone. Paint buildup also may add thickness to the door or frame, preventing a tight fit. To correct the problem, plane down the edges of the door.

When a cabinet element refuses to work smoothly, it usually takes only a few minutes to find out why.

Operate the drawer or door, and take a close look at what's happening. Is a drawer glide binding? A

hinge sagging? A catch refusing to catch? The photographs opposite show remedies.

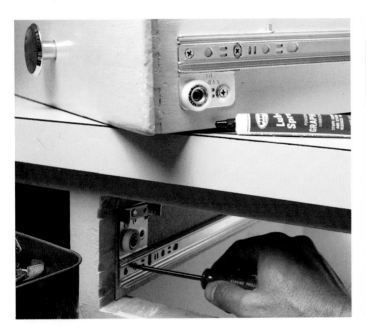

When a drawer with metal side glides sticks, remove the drawer and thoroughly clean both glides. Apply powdered graphite or silicone lubricant. Make sure the screws holding the glides are tight and secure.

Over the years, wooden center glides can become rough and worn. First smooth the glide with sandpaper, then rub it with crayon or candle wax to help eliminate friction when the drawer slides.

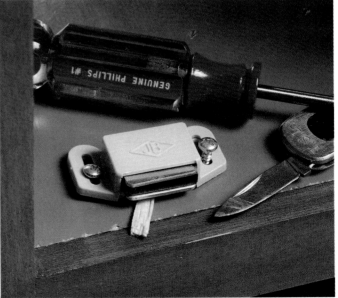

Loose hinge screws cause cabinet doors to sag. If the screw holes have enlarged, tightening the screws won't help. To reduce the size of the hole, insert a toothpick coated with glue and reinsert the screw.

To work properly, magnetic catches must be in near-perfect alignment. Screws let you adjust a catch back and forth. A sliver of wood, forced underneath as a shim, lets you adjust vertical alignment.

REPAIRING
FAUCETS
AND TOILETS

Look for signs of corrosion or worn O-rings on the assembly of a modern cartridge-type stem faucet.

Dripping faucets and gurgling toilets are water tortures you don't have to endure. In most cases, the cause of the problem is wear on rubber seals that stop the flow of water.

Stem faucets, those with separate hot and cold water controls, work by compression. With older versions, turning the handle rotates a threaded stem that presses a rubber washer into a seat at the base of the stem. More modern stem faucets may have a stem cartridge like the one held in the photo *at upper right*. A rubber O-ring slips onto the cartridge to keep water from flowing up the stem.

To repair a stem faucet, shut off water to the faucet, pry up the decorative piece on the top of each handle, back out the screw in the handle, and remove any decorative covering around the faucet's base. At the base, you'll find a nut. Turn this out, then lift or unscrew the stem. Clean the stem with fine steel wool, and replace any worn washers, O-rings, or seals at the bottom of the stem. If new rubber doesn't stop a cartridge faucet from dripping, replace the cartridge.

Also run your finger around the metal seat at the faucet base. If it feels rough or pitted, you'll need to smooth it with a specialized hand tool called a seat grinder.

If you have a single-lever rotating-ball faucet, such as the one shown *at lower right,* check for worn O-rings. In addition, after removing the ball, insert a pencil into the doughnut-shape rubber seals at the

If the water flow from a faucet spout is constricted, remove the aerator and clean out debris or mineral deposits from the screen.

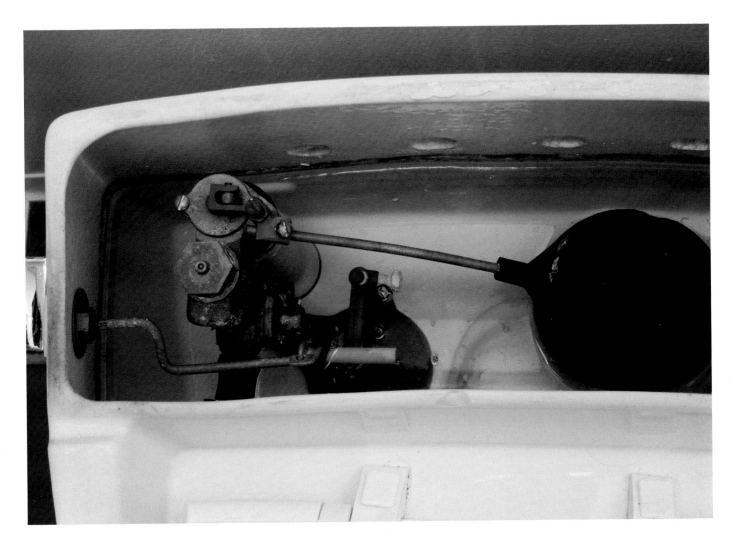

base. Pull out the pencil and a seal and its spring will come out, too. If the seals and springs are worn, replace them; if the ball is corroded, replace it, too.

Inside a flush tank

With a toilet that won't stop running, remove the tank cover and observe what happens when the toilet is flushed.

Tripping the handle on a toilet activates a lever that lifts a ball at the bottom of the tank, opening a passage between the tank and the bowl. Water rushes into the bowl, carrying

waste down the toilet trap into the drain line. At the top of the tank, a large float ball lowers as the water level in the tank drops. When the water level drops to a certain point, the rod attached to the float trips the flush valve. This in turn causes the ball at the bottom of the tank to settle back in its seat; at the same time the valve lets in water to fill the tank. When the float reaches the top of the tank again, the flush valve shuts off.

Reach into the tank and lift up the float. Raising it should close off the toilet's flush valve. If this silences the toilet, try bending the supporting rod *downward* to increase pressure on the flush valve linkage as the float rises. An old ball may not float properly; replace it with a new one.

If raising the float rod doesn't shut off the flow, the flush valve is probably faulty. Consult a plumbing guide if you'd like to try repairing the valve yourself.

Sometimes the problem lies at the bottom of the tank with the tank ball and its seat. To correct this, shut off the water supply to the tank, and flush the toilet to drain the tank. Check the wire stem that protrudes from the ball. If the wire is bent, straighten it and see if the ball seats better. Or try adjusting the guide arm that connects to the top of the wire stem. Also examine the ball itself, and replace it, if necessary. To ensure that the ball fits tightly into its seat, scrub the edges of the seat with steel wool.

85

CLEARING STOPPED-UP DRAINS

When a kitchen or bathroom sink drains sluggishly or clogs completely, debris is trapped somewhere in the drainage system. The location of the blockage determines what action you need to take. (Caution: If a drain is completely clogged, don't use a chemical drain opener; if it isn't successful, your original problem will be compounded by a sink and pipes filled with caustic solution.)

Start from the top by examining the strainer or stopper. Kitchen sink strainer baskets simply lift out. Bathroom stoppers usually lift straight out or require a twist before lifting. If this doesn't release the stopper, look under the sink; you may need to disengage a pivot rod. Once the stopper is free, clean away debris.

If the stopper isn't the culprit, reach for a *plunger,* also known as a force cup, or plumber's friend. The box opposite explains how to use a plunger.

If plunging for at least five minutes fails to remedy the problem, move from the sink to the pipes below it. At this stage, what you do depends on the tools you have on hand. *Augers,* a sampling of which are pictured *at lower right,* have cranks or motors at one end and stiff springs at the other to bore through blockages.

To thread an auger through pipes, insert the spring and crank the handle. As you crank, the auger travels deeper into the pipe. When the crank becomes hard to turn, you've reached the blockage. At this point, keep cranking while also pushing and pulling the auger back and forth. This will either snag the blockage so you can pull it out, or break it up so you can flush it away.

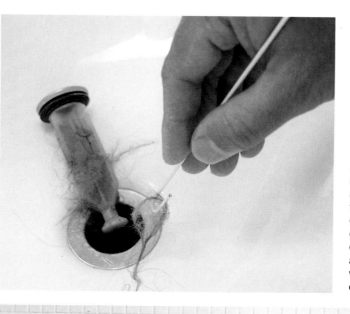

Often you can use a coat hanger to remove debris trapped in the stem of a bathroom stopper.

Augers and snakes come in a variety of lengths and diameters. Below, clockwise from the left, are: a heavy-duty auger powered by an electric drill, two 5½-foot drain and trap augers, and a 25-foot snake that can be worked through tight drain openings.

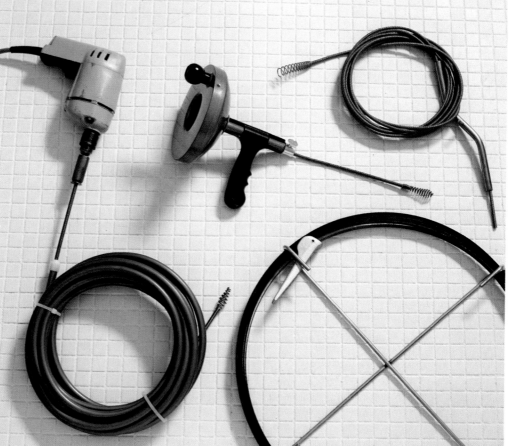

The plunger pictured below works best on toilets and sinks with curved bottoms. For flat-bottom sinks or tubs, use a plain cup plunger without a projection in the center.

A bent metal sleeve converts one of the drain augers shown opposite into a closet auger. The sleeve directs the auger through the toilet's trap. You also can buy augers designed specifically for toilets.

If you don't own an auger, a wire coat hanger will sometimes do the trick. Straighten the hanger and bend one end into a small hook. Next, put a deep bucket beneath the trap and open the trap. Some traps have a nutlike cleanout fitting at the bottom. With others, such as the U-shape trap shown *at right,* you'll need to remove a section of the pipe. Once you've gained access to the trap, work the hooked end of the hanger into each side of the trap and try to snag the obstruction and pull it out.

To unblock a toilet, first try plunging. If plunging doesn't work, you'll need to resort to an auger. Because toilets have built-in traps that angle upward, you'll need a *closet auger,* which has a sharp bend at the top. This type, pictured *at top right,* also has a handle to keep your hands clean.

A PLUMBER'S FRIEND

Plungers work by building up water pressure inside a drain, so if the sink you're working on has an overflow, block it with rags. Remove the stopper or strainer and be sure water covers the plunger cup. Place the cup over the drain opening (petroleum jelly on the rim improves the seal) and pump up and down several times. After a forceful down stroke, pull the plunger up as hard as you can. Repeat until the fixture unclogs.

To remove a trap, loosen the slip nuts securing the trap. You may want to wrap tape around the jaws of your wrench or pliers to protect plating. After a half-turn or so, unscrew the nuts by hand.

KEEPING THINGS CLEAN AND SANITARY

When sliding shower doors stick, the cause is often dirt and soap residue that have accumulated in the track. To get doors sliding freely **again, scrub the track with an old toothbrush and mild abrasive cleanser. After the track is clean and dry, apply silicone lubricant.**

Even with conscientious, regular cleaning, the edges of metal-rimmed sinks can trap dirt. Scrape it away **with a toothpick. Avoid using a metal implement, which could scratch the metal rim.**

Kitchens and baths are messy, high-traffic, high-activity zones, and keeping them clean often seems like an endless battle. A proper arsenal of cleansers and implements, along with some resolve, will help you stay on top of things.

The chart opposite details what you'll need to stock for cleaning a variety of surfaces. If you make any new purchases, save the manufacturer's care information and combine it with the suggestions on the chart. It's a good idea to test any strong cleaners in a small, inconspicuous spot before proceeding.

You'll note that regular care often involves nothing more than a damp sponge and mild detergent. Always start cleaning any surface with the gentlest substance you can; you'll need to tackle some stains with strong abrasives, but turn to them as last resorts. Even the toughest surfaces eventually deteriorate under an onslaught of repeated rough cleaning.

In addition to brushes and mops bought specifically for cleaning, save items such as old toothbrushes, shoe brushes, clothing discards made of absorbent materials, and plastic containers, especially ones with spray tops.

In a large house, you may find it most efficient to duplicate items you use in both the kitchen and bath, so supplies are stored right where you need them.

The photographs *at left* give information about cleaning a couple of tough spots; the box at right tells about recaulking around fixtures such as bathtubs.

CAULKING AROUND FIXTURES

To seal the junctures where fixtures meet walls, you need a flexible caulking compound. Periodically examine the edges of sinks, showers, and tubs, and recaulk when you find crumbling grout or loosened caulk. Scrape out unsound material with a screwdriver or the point of a can opener, then brush or vacuum clean. Seal the gap with one of two kinds of caulk.

• *Vinyl latex* is easy to apply; its surface can be smoothed with a wet finger. Once dry, the caulk is water-resistant and can be painted. It's moderately expensive.

• *Silicone* caulk is long lasting and highly elastic, qualities you pay substantially more for. Also, paint will not adhere to some silicones.

With either type, make sure that the caulk resists mildew.

Ranging from most to least expensive, caulk is available in squeeze tubes, in cartridges that slip into half-barrel caulking guns, or in bulk containers from which you load full-barrel guns.

To apply caulk, snip the nozzle of the tube at an angle. The closer to the tip you cut, the narrower the bead of caulk. Aim to apply a smooth coved bed that will channel water away from the wall into the fixture.

CLEANING KITCHEN AND BATH SURFACES

	REGULAR CARE	SPOT/STAIN REMOVAL	SPECIAL TREATMENTS
COUNTERS			
Plastic laminate	Wipe with a damp sponge and mild detergent solution.	Try a paste of baking soda and water to draw out stains.	Protect with appliance wax; avoid abrasive cleaners.
Wood	Damp-sponge; dry. Avoid too much water.	Wipe with a 50% ammonia solution; use fine steel wool on scratches.	To prevent oiled wood from drying out, reoil periodically.
Hard-surface tile	Wipe with sudsy water; dry with a soft cloth.	Use a degreaser on oily spots and special cleaner on tile grout.	Apply creamy liquid wax for an easy-to-clean finish.
FIXTURES AND APPLIANCES			
Baked-on enamel	Wipe with mild detergent; rinse.	Use chlorine bleach on stains; try a mild abrasive and a nylon brush on soap or mineral deposits.	Treat gently; abrasives will eventually remove the finish.
Fiberglass	Wipe with a soft cloth; dry. Never use abrasive cleansers.	Try white automotive compound to remove occasional stains.	Restore shine with liquid or paste auto wax.
Metal	Use mild liquid soap and water; wipe dry.	Use an abrasive cleanser to remove most stains.	Try automotive chrome cleaner on rust or tarnish.
Vitreous china	Use a mild liquid detergent; rinse and dry.	Remove mineral buildup or stains with cream of tartar paste.	Strong abrasives can permanently etch the surface.
Porcelain	Scrub with detergent and hot water.	Use a mild scouring powder or chlorine bleach solution.	On tough stains, try a paste of cream of tartar and hydrogen peroxide.
FLOORS			
Resilient	Dust-mop, sweep, or vacuum. Damp-mop as needed.	Scrub with mild detergent or appliance cleaner/wax.	Use liquid wax on waxables and special dressing on no-wax types.
Wood	Dry-mop; damp-mop. Avoid excess water.	Sanding and refinishing may be necessary.	Use solvent-base polish to clean and wax. Buff.
Tile/slate	Dust-mop; vacuum; damp-mop as needed.	Use cleanser or washing soda on greasy spots.	Finish unprotected tiles with oil-base sealer.
WALLS AND CABINETS			
Paint/wall coverings	Wash in small sections with detergent solution.	Use degreaser on oily spots or stains.	Use wallpaper cleaner on nonwashable coverings.
Prefinished wood	Dust; use a wax- or oil-type polish; wipe with the grain.	Treat sticky, oily spots with appliance cleaner/wax.	Avoid using too much water on wood. Always wipe dry.
Ceramic tile	Wipe clean with a mild detergent and water solution.	Use baking soda paste or grout cleaner; blot and rinse.	Avoid abrasive cleansers.

KEEPING
WATER FLOWING

Most of us rarely think about the water systems so vital to kitchens and baths—until something goes wrong. When that happens, it's usually just after hardware stores have closed, or just before company is to arrive. Drain problems, especially, tend to occur at inopportune moments. Your best defense is to establish house rules about what should and shouldn't go down drains, and to set up a kit with basic plumbing tools and parts so you're prepared for the inevitable.

Save some empty covered cans and waxed cartons under the kitchen sink and use them to dispose of grease, coffee grinds, and other potential cloggers that shouldn't go into a drain. If a drain tends to be sluggish, periodic use of a chemical drain opener may keep it flowing freely.

Disposers: special kinds of drains

Garbage disposers, which grind waste before letting it pass down the drain, can handle most food waste, including bones, coffee grounds, and rinds, but avoid putting in fibrous wastes such as corn husks and artichokes. Hard materials, such as small bones and ice cubes, actually are beneficial. As they knock against the sides of the grinding chamber they help dislodge grease so it can pass through the system.

If a disposer drain line does clog, handle it as you would an ordinary kitchen drain. With a bucket underneath, disconnect the trap and clean it out. For blockages beyond the trap, work an auger down the drainpipe.

When a disposer jams, it's usually because a hard object, such as a piece of flatware, has accidentally fallen in. Shut off the power and remove the splashguard so you can view the grinding chamber. Once you've located the obstruction, use a broom or mop handle—never your hand—to pry against the grinder until it rotates and releases the trapped object.

Some disposers are designed so that you can insert an allen wrench into a hole in the bottom of the unit, then work the wrench back and forth to dislodge a blockage.

To keep blades sharp, you can purchase a special abrasive product that you pour into the disposer periodically.

Tools of the trade

Minor repairs and maintenance go more smoothly if you have the right tools and supplies on hand. Assemble a basic kit with the following items:

• *A rubber plunger* or *force cup* for dislodging blockages in drains and toilets.

• *A plumber's snake* or *auger* for sink drains. If you frequently have trouble with toilets, also include a *closet auger*.

• *An assortment of wrenches*. Start with a 10- and an 18-inch pipe wrench, a smaller adjustable-end wrench, and an allen wrench.

• *A selection of screwdrivers*, both standard and Phillips. Also include some offset blades for getting into tight places.

• Whenever you buy small items like *screws, nuts,* and *washers,* buy several, so you always have an assortment of sizes available. Also buy more than one of items such as *O-rings, toilet tank balls,* and *magnets* or *rollers* for cabinet catches. These items aren't expensive, but shopping for the exact sizes you need can be time-consuming.

Treating water

The chart on page 89 explains how to keep kitchen and bath

surfaces clean. Depending on where you live and whether your water comes from a municipal source or a private well, you also may encounter some vexing cleaning problems caused by the water itself.

• *Hard water* contains excessive amounts of calcium and magnesium. Combined with soaps or detergents, these minerals inhibit cleaning action. Soaps refuse to lather or foam and leave sticky films or curdlike deposits. This residue irritates sensitive skin, clings to fixtures in unsightly rings, and makes clothes washing difficult.

In addition, hard water allows corrosive scale to build up inside your plumbing system. Scale in pipes, water heaters, faucets, and appliances makes them work less efficiently and wear out more quickly.

Water softening units combat hard water by capturing excess minerals in a column of plastic resin beads. The resin is then bathed in a salt solution that removes the minerals and flushes them away. Then the resin is rinsed of salt, so another cycle can begin.

• Water with a *high iron content* causes reddish rust discolorations on fixtures, especially around drains. To eliminate this problem, you need an oxidizing filtering system instead of, or in addition to, a water softener.

• Other filtering devices use chlorine, activated charcoal, cellulose elements, and plastic membranes to remove manganese, hydrogen sulfide, salt, and pesticides.

If you suspect water impurities, have a county agency or private laboratory analyze a sample. You may need a combination of devices to correct the problem.

When to call a professional

Most homeowners can handle the routine plumbing chores discussed in this chapter. For some problems, however, you'll want to call in a licensed plumber or a drain and sewer cleaning service.

Unless you're skilled at pipe fitting, you'll probably want to have a plumber replace leaking or damaged pipes, or add runs to new fixtures and appliances.

When it comes to drain problems, try to remedy those close to fixtures yourself, and resort to a professional for blockages farther down the line. To determine where the trouble is, turn on a faucet at each sink, tub, or other fixture, but don't flush any toilets. If only one fixture is clogged, the problem is in or near that fixture's drain. Fortunately, most blockages occur in fixture drains. If two or more fixtures are stopped up, something is blocking a main drain, which connects fixture drains to the main waste pipe. If none of the drains work, the obstruction is either near the point where a main drain connects to the sewer drain, or in the sewer drain itself.

A hand-operated auger will clear fixture drains and also let you get partway down a main drain. For blockages farther down, you'll need a professional drain and sewer cleaner, who'll bring in heavy-duty power equipment.

Drain and sewer cleaning does not require a plumbing license, so these services are less expensive than calling in a plumber. Some licensed plumbers do drain cleaning, but you'll be paying for expertise you may not need.

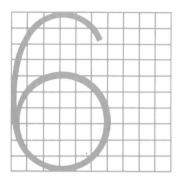

MAJOR APPLIANCES

Basic appliances are expensive—and vital to convenience and comfort in most contemporary households. Once you've selected, paid for, and installed major appliances, you can expect years of trouble-free performance. Neglect and misuse can undermine reliability, however, so take the time to give these vital household helpers the regular preventive care they need and deserve. This chapter, in combination with your collection of manufacturer-supplied owner's manuals (which you should always save), gives useful pointers about appliance care, maintenance, and troubleshooting.

COOKING EQUIPMENT

The top surface of a gas range lifts easily. This allows you to clean the burners and check the pilot light and flame intensity.

Wiping up everyday spills will go a long way toward keeping your range clean. But at some point after regular, prolonged use, serious cleaning will be in order. Gas ranges, in particular, become grimy under the best of circumstances. Fortunately, all ranges are easy to put back into original condition, because their parts easily dismantle for cleaning.

To cook properly, a gas flame should be blue, with a light blue tip. If the flame is part yellow, or soot collects under the pot at frequent intervals, too little air is mixing with the gas and proper combustion isn't taking place. If the flame is noisy or floats above the burner, too much air is mixing in. To correct this, adjust the burner's air shutter, located at the front of the range, just behind the control knob. Here, you'll find a screw. Loosen it and turn or slide the shutter until you get a satisfactory flame. Then tighten the screw to secure the shutter.

Safety pointers

Like all home appliances, gas ranges are designed to be safely operated by the general public. That doesn't mean you can be careless, however. Don't smoke near a range when working on it. Use a flashlight, not a match, to peer into dark corners. Don't move the stove away from the wall; call a repairman if an inaccessible part needs adjusting.

If you smell gas, make sure the pilot light is lit. If you still smell gas, turn off the gas-supply valve and call a repairman. Do not turn on anything electrical, even the kitchen light switch, until the leak is repaired. Sparking could ignite the gas. While you're waiting, open the windows to ventilate the room.

To improve burner performance, unscrew the burner retainer screw and lift it out. Clean clogged ignition ports with a toothpick and wash the burner in a solution of ammonia and water.

To recalibrate an oven that burns or underbakes, pull off the knob and adjust the small screw underneath. Check with an oven thermometer, then readjust, as necessary.

Heating elements lift out for cleaning or replacing. Remove the reflector pan. Unscrew the element, then pull it out. Use a wood or plastic implement to scrape off any burnt food.

Electric ranges don't generate as much dirt during normal use as gas ranges do, but they require regular maintenance all the same.

One of the most common problems with electric ranges is burners that don't heat up properly. Sometimes, defective elements are at fault. To check a surface heating element, set the control to "high" and see if the burner glows within seconds. If it doesn't, turn off the range and examine the dead element. If there are marks on its surface, replace the element. The photograph *at upper right* shows how to do this.

Besides the elements, the leads and the heating control could be at fault, as well as the terminals the burners plug into. Worn-out, corroded terminals lose their ability to conduct electricity. This can cause both the burners and the oven to stop working. After turning off the power, check for burnt terminals. Discoloration or burn marks tell the tale. Replace the part to which the terminal is joined and the charred lead. You can use a volt-ohm meter to check the leads to the element. The terminal block is usually at the back of the range.

The oven heating element should glow quickly when turned on. If it doesn't, remove the element and test it with a volt-ohm meter set to the RX1 setting. It should read between 15 and 30 ohms. If the reading is higher, replace the oven element, as shown in the photograph *at lower right*. As with gas ranges, you have to observe basic safety precautions when you investigate an electric range. Whenever you work on one, turn off the power before you do anything else. Either remove the fuse to the range's circuit or trip the circuit breaker.

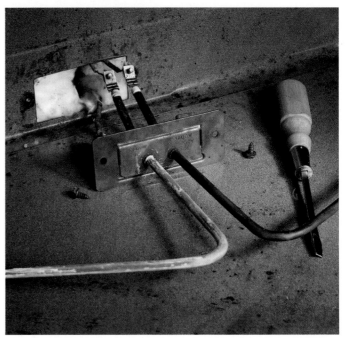

Test the oven and broiler elements. If one doesn't glow promptly, it needs replacing. If neither works, the problem probably originates elsewhere. To replace the heating element of an electric oven, first turn off the power to the range, then remove the screws that hold the element to the back of the oven panel. Pull the element several inches toward you, disconnect the leads from the terminals, then lift the element out. Replace the defective element with a new one obtained from the manufacturer.

WASHERS, DRYERS, AND DISHWASHERS

If clothes are still damp after completing a normal drying cycle, a clogged exhaust vent may be con-stricting air movement. Remove any obstruction in the vent outside the laundry room wall.

Remove lint and compacted fuzz from the vent hose line regularly. A vacuum cleaner hose collects lint caught behind crevices and ridges. After vacuuming, reconnect the vent hose.

Clean the lint trap of your dryer often. A vacuum cleaner brush will dislodge lint stuck to the screen. Models vary, so read the owner's manual to determine the location of the screen.

Replace worn or broken drum belts in a washer or dryer. Check the belt for loose tension, then turn the drum. If it turns easily, the belt is broken. Unplug the machine, lift the drum a bit, and replace the belt.

Remove the vanes of an agitator by unscrewing the top, then clean and polish the mechanism to remove lint and encrusted detergent. An old toothbrush is useful for getting into corners.

If a gasket is hard or cracked, replace it. First, remove the old gasket, which may be mounted on the door or the cabinet. Then, insert a new gasket, making sure the door doesn't press against it too tightly.

Many of the problems that occur with washers and dryers can be solved without expert assistance. Common and easily corrected problems include overloaded machines, unbalanced loads, clogged filters and lint traps, unplugged power cords, uneven positioning on the floor, blown fuses, clogged intakes and drains, and loose electrical connections. See the photographs and captions *opposite, above,* and *at right* for more solutions to common problems.

Acute problems aside, a lot depends on good maintenance—that is, using the appliance properly. Too much or too little detergent, for example, can cause problems. Underloading, although it won't interfere with the machine's function, isn't energy-efficient. Smooth operation is something you won't get if there's a loose object or other obstruction inside a washer or dryer. Common sense applies, too. Don't let young children operate or play with an appliance, both for their own safety and for the machine's well-being.

Dishwashers
Perhaps the most common problem with dishwashers comes from expecting too much from them. Be sure to remove food and grease from plates and utensils before you put them into the machine; otherwise you risk clogging the drain, pumps, or machinery.

In addition, clean the holes in the sprayer regularly so they don't become clogged with detergent residue and food particles. If the pump becomes clogged, turn off the power and remove the spray and strainer. Then remove any food or obstacles from the pump assembly underneath.

Washers and dryers must be level to prevent excessive vibration. (A pan of water set on top will show if the appliance tilts.) Use a wrench to adjust the locknut leveler screws or legs under the machine.

REFRIGERATORS AND FREEZERS

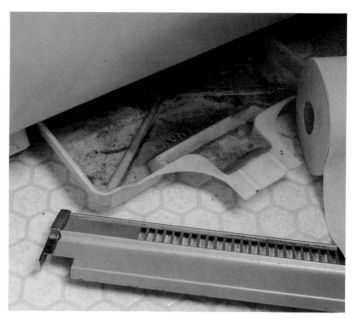

Clean the interior of a refrigerator or freezer regularly. Wipe the walls, shelves, and bins with a solution of baking soda and water. This cleans without abrading and also removes odors.

A refrigerator drip pan can breed germs and odors if it's not clean. Remove the base grille and pull out the pan to wash it. Vacuum any dust under the refrigerator. Reposition the pan solidly. Replace a leaky pan.

Energy bills can go way up if a door gasket is defective. Check for airtightness by inserting a piece of paper or a new dollar bill in the door. If you feel little or no resistance as you pull it out, replace the gasket.

Condenser coils, located in back of or under the refrigerator, collect dust, and when they get dusty, the refrigerator has to work harder than it should. Use a vacuum brush attachment to clean the coils.

KEEPING APPLIANCES CLEAN

The more conscientious you are about daily maintenance, the easier it will be to keep appliance surfaces looking their best. Whatever the material, certain general points are worth keeping in mind.

- Always wipe up spills right away.
- Avoid abrasive cleaners and rough scouring pads.
- Apply appliance wax occasionally to keep dirt from adhering to surfaces.
- Follow manufacturers' care instructions.

Use appliance touch-up paint to hide chips and nicks. This paint also prevents rusting. Some new appliances have a slightly textured surface that makes smudges and fingerprints less noticeable.

Caring for common materials

Although the general rule of "Never use abrasives" applies to virtually all materials, some nonabrasive cleaning agents are better for certain surfaces than for others.

- For *glass panels*, use glass cleaner or a solution of baking soda and water. The latter must be thoroughly rinsed off to avoid clouding.
- Sponge *plastic and plastic laminate* with a gentle dish detergent.
- Wipe *baked-on enamel* with mild liquid detergent, then rinse.
- Clean *painted metal* with mild liquid cleaner.
- Use soapy water, not ammonia, for *aluminum*.
- Clean *stainless steel* with mild detergent, glass cleaner, or special-purpose stainless-steel cleaner. Vinegar removes stains; olive oil keeps the steel from spotting quite so readily.
- Use metal cleaner or chrome polish for *chrome*.

CLEANING INSIDE APPLIANCES

APPLIANCE	REGULAR CARE	SPECIAL POINTERS
REFRIGERATOR	Wash with baking soda solution; then rinse.	Use vinegar to remove mildew. Put mineral oil on door gaskets to prevent cracking.
DISHWASHER	Interiors are self-cleaning in operation. Check periodically for a clogged air gap over the sink and a clogged drain or sprayer.	Clean the drain with baking soda solution. Surround a clogged drain with baking soda, pour on boiling water, let it sit, then drain. Never use drain cleaners. They corrode aluminum and rubber parts.
WASHER	It is self-cleaning, except for the lint trap.	After dyeing clothes in a washer, clean the drum by running the empty machine with bleach and detergent.
DRYER	No need to clean the interior. Clean lint out of the vent hose, vent, and filter.	Check the drum occasionally to see if it's worn and rough.
DISPOSER	The works are self-cleaning in operation. If the disposer is sluggish, grind some ice cubes to clean it.	Avoid chemical or abrasive cleaners. If cleaning really is necessary, use an enzymatic cleanser that's labeled disposer-safe.
OVEN HOOD	Wash aluminum mesh filters in the dishwasher or sink every two weeks.	Check that the deactivated charcoal behind filters is not contaminated with grease. If it is, replace it.
RANGE/OVEN	Soak gas burners in soapy water or an ammonia solution. Scrub them with a stiff brush. Use oven cleaner, detergent, or ammonia cleaner in the oven.	Don't let ammonia oven cleaner sit in a gas oven overnight. The pilot light could ignite fumes.

TROUBLESHOOTING CHECKLIST

No matter how carefully you may treat your appliances, there are bound to be times when they don't perform to expectations. For that reason, these two pages contain a checklist of common problems and commonsense solutions, organized by appliance.

Refrigerator

• If your refrigerator cools poorly, see if the freezer needs to be defrosted. Check for a worn door gasket, out-of-kilter hinges that let the door sag or tilt, and dirty condenser coils. One or more of these conditions could be the culprit.

• If your refrigerator is noisy, try repositioning the drain pan so it doesn't rattle. Also check to see if objects are striking the condenser fan.

• If your refrigerator smells, see if the interior needs cleaning or defrosting. Also check the drain pan under the appliance: It, too, may need cleaning. Finally, check for clogged drains inside the refrigerator.

• If your refrigerator sweats or drips in hot weather, check the temperature control to make sure it's not set too cold. Condensation can be caused by too big a drop in temperature from the inside to the outside. Also turn the dial to the "damp" setting if it has one.

• If the contents of a freezer stick to its interior surface, try wiping the surface with alcohol, after defrosting.

Washer

• If the tub doesn't fill, try unkinking the water inlet hose, unclogging the inlet valve, or opening water faucets more.

• If the machine doesn't spin, or spins poorly, try balancing the load better. You may need to remove some items if the machine is overloaded. Check to see if there's a defective lid safety switch; look for a loose drive belt or clothing jammed under the basket. Be sure the drain is clear so water can leave the tub freely.

• If the machine does not drain, check for kinked water inlet hoses, oversudsing, a clogged house drain, or a jammed drain pump.

• If the machine leaks, check for oversudsing, leaks or cracks in the seal, worn or kinked hoses, or worn hose washers.

• If the machine seems excessively noisy, check to see that the machine isn't overloaded. Rebalance the load, if necessary. If this doesn't eliminate the noise, perhaps you should level the base.

• If the machine tears clothes, check for a rough basket, broken agitator vane, overloading, or too little water to wash the load properly. Too much bleach also may be the culprit.

• If the washer is installed in a closet or alcove, be sure that there's enough air space between the machine and the walls for adequate ventilation.

Sometimes, it's important for safety reasons to know about potential trouble before you have even a hint of it. Here are two serious safety tips.

• If you haven't used any hot water for two weeks or more, check for explosive hydrogen gas that could have formed in the water heater before you run either your washer or your dishwasher. Do this by running hot water in a faucet a few minutes. Do not smoke while doing this.

• If you are washing garments that have cleaning solvent on them, be sure to rinse them thoroughly first in cold water, so they won't explode in the heat of the washer's hot-water cycle.

Dryer

• If the drum does not turn, check for a broken drum belt, broken idler spring, or lint that's obstructing the drum.

• If the dryer does not heat, check for a clogged lint screen, a faulty thermostat, a faulty timer, or a faulty heater.

• If clothes dry poorly, you may be overloading the dryer. If that's not the problem, see if the lint screen is clogged. Other possible solutions: Unkink the vent hose, clean the vent, or replace a leaking door seal.

• If the dryer is noisy, check for a loose object in the drum. If you don't find one, see if the problem is a worn drum belt, loose blower, or obstructed blower duct.

• If the dryer tears clothes, check the drum to see if it has become rough with age and use.

Dishwasher

• If the dishwasher does not fill, first be sure the water is turned on. Then, check to see if the float is dirty, stuck, or out of position. If the float seems stuck, remove it, check for any obstructions, and replace it. If the float isn't the problem, see if the inlet valve screen is clogged.

• If the dishwasher doesn't drain properly, check for a clogged strainer, pump, or drain valve. Also see if the drain hose is kinked.

• If dishes don't come out clean, check the water temperature. To do this, turn on the hot-water faucet closest to the machine. Hold a cooking thermometer under the flow. If the temperature is lower than that recommended by the dishwasher manufacturer, consider turning up your water heater's thermostat. Many newer dishwashers have preheaters that boost the temperature of incoming water, regardless of your water heater's setting. Other causes for poor cleaning include a clogged strainer, sprayer, or detergent dispenser, and old, lumpy detergent that doesn't dissolve properly.

• If the dishwasher leaks or overflows, check the door gasket; it may be damaged or loose. Also check for a clogged inlet valve, loose hose clamp, or defective pump seal. See if the dishwasher is level; adjust the legs, if necessary. And be sure you're not using too much detergent: Oversudsing causes leaking. Check the cutoff switch, too. It may be stuck or need replacing.

• If the dishwasher is too noisy, see if there's a loose object in the bottom of the tub. Also, try loading dishes so the sprayer arm can move freely, and avoid running water for other purposes during the washing cycle, so the machine fills adequately. Check for a defective inlet valve, too.

Range

• If an electric surface element does not heat, it may be defective or the lead may be worn out.

• If an electric oven does not heat, check for a defective heating element or thermostat.

• If a gas burner does not work, check for an unlit pilot light, a clogged burner, or poor gas-air mixture.

• If a gas oven heats poorly, check to see if the pilot flame is set too low or the flame switch is faulty.

• If your oven burns food, see if the exhaust vent needs unblocking. Also check the oven temperature with an oven thermometer; it may be hotter than the temperature setting and the thermostat may need adjusting, as explained on page 94.
• If the oven bakes unevenly, check for a defective gasket on the oven door.

Disposer

• If the machine doesn't run at all, see if the overload protector has tripped off. If the motor hums but the machine doesn't run, check for a jammed flywheel.
• If the machine jams, try the reverse switch, or shut off the unit and use a broomstick or special tool from the manufacturer to reverse the blades. Remove any jammed objects with tongs.
• If the motor starts but stops, check for a worn cam or stopper switch.
• If the disposer is clogged but not jammed, try grinding ice cubes sprinkled with disposer-safe cleanser, or grind orange or lemon peels with hot running water.
• If the machine grinds slowly, try running more water through the machine when it's operating. See, too, if any ungrindable material has been put into the disposer. If these two suggestions don't help, check for a broken flywheel or dull shredder ring.
• If the disposer drains poorly, try running more water through it when you're operating it, or look for a clogged drain line, a broken flywheel, or a dull shredder ring.
• If the disposer leaks water, check for a loose flange on the drain gasket, a poor seal at the sink gasket, or a poor seal between the hopper and the shredder housing.

• If the disposer seems too noisy, see if there is a foreign object (such as a piece of metal) in it. Then check for loose mounting screws, a broken flywheel, or a defective motor.
• If grease collects on surfaces, be sure to always use cold water when you run the disposer. Cold water hardens grease, making it possible for the machine to grind and dispose of it. Hot water just melts grease, defeating the purpose of the machine.

Trash compactor

• If you've just changed the bag and the unit refuses to operate, the bucket probably has been installed improperly. Compactors usually have two safety switches—one activated by the door (so you can't open it when the compactor is running), the other by the bucket (so you can't operate it without the bucket in place).
• The door won't close? Look behind and under the bucket. Trash may have fallen back there and need to be removed.
• If the door opens only a few inches, or not at all, a can or other item has probably wedged itself between the top of the ram and the motor unit. To get at the problem, you may need to remove the door from its hinges—as explained in the installation manual—then dismount the bucket from the door. After you've removed the obstruction and reinstalled the bucket and door, turning on the unit will lift the ram back into position.
   Like most appliances, compactors pose a few potential safety hazards if they're not used properly. Here are some tips to keep in mind.

• Never permit small children to operate a compactor. Most have a safety key—sometimes the control knob—that can be removed easily and kept out of the reach of children.
• Don't push trash into the bucket with your hands or feet. Broken glass or other sharp debris could cause a nasty cut.
• Check the manufacturer's instructions and familiarize yourself with what the unit can and cannot handle. Never compact flammable materials, toxic chemicals, or aerosol cans. Most compactors can crush glass, but be warned that shards can easily slice through the bag when you're removing it. For this reason, hold the bag well away from your body.

Range hoods

• If you have a ductless recirculating hood that isn't controlling grease, try running it five minutes before cooking. Keep it going until 10 minutes after you are through.
• If the filters from a recirculating ductless hood have not been cleaned regularly, check for grease contamination on the deactivated charcoal inside. Replace the charcoal and clean the filter as necessary.
• If you have a ducted hood, clean the filter regularly to maintain its efficiency.
• If the disposer is connected to the same drain line as the dishwasher, be sure they aren't operated at the same time. Run the disposer after the dishwasher, to clear away food particles washed from dishes.
• If the disposer drains slowly, try clearing it with hot water and half a cup of washing soda, vinegar, or ammonia.

BEFORE YOU CALL FOR SERVICE

Many a service call and its charges can be saved by doing a little preliminary investigation before calling a repairman. The checklist at left identifies some specific problems and their solutions, but often the problem is more basic.
• Make sure that the appliance is plugged in and the electrical current is flowing. Try plugging a lamp into the same outlet. If it doesn't light, the problem is electrical and the appliance is probably all right.
• Check the instruction manual to be sure that the appliance has been installed and operated according to the manufacturer's specifications.
• Check for any mechanical obstructions that might be interfering with operation.
• Check all knobs and controls to be sure that, in cleaning, nothing has been turned off or turned to an automatic setting that overrides the "on" switch.
• Don't touch a machine that sparks, smokes, or gives the slightest shock. Make sure no water is touching electrical parts.
   And remember: Always turn the power off before inspecting any piece of equipment, and don't reach into an appliance until it has stopped spinning.

SETTING UP YOUR OWN APPLIANCE MAINTENANCE AGENDA

Keeping up with routine maintenance for appliances, like most other household areas, is mostly a matter of breaking the jobs down into manageable chunks. The schedule of care suggested here isn't absolute. What you do, how much, and when depends on the amount of cooking and laundry you, and your appliances, are responsible for. Use these suggestions as guidelines, not deadlines.

Some things need to be done almost constantly—cleanup chores to keep spills from hardening into a hard-to-remove residue, for example. Other tasks only need to be done occasionally, to assure an appliance's smooth operation. Be flexible but conscientious: The idea is to take good care of these helpers so they'll continue to simplify *your* life.

The following tips are divided into daily, weekly, monthly, seasonal, and annual categories. They range from simple good-usage practices to semi-repair tasks that a moderately handy homeowner can reasonably and safely attempt.

Daily care
• First, a safety rule: Don't let children play with or operate appliances. This safety tip has a maintenance fringe benefit, as well, because an appliance that doesn't suffer misuse is less likely to break.
• Wipe up all food spilled on or inside appliances.
• Store food properly in the refrigerator to prevent spills and odors.
• Use the garbage disposer properly, so it doesn't jam. Operate after dumping food, rather than letting garbage pile up inside it.
• Use the range vent hood consistently to control grease buildup in your kitchen.
• Use an aluminum foil shield under anything that is likely to bubble over in the oven. Be careful not to block the oven air vent, however.
• Do not drag heavy objects across appliances or drop things on them.
• For best appearance, wipe off water spots on stainless steel surfaces.
• Keep refrigerator contents organized so you don't run up energy bills or overwork the motor by having the door open too long while you hunt for items.
• Use the proper amount of detergent in appliances.
• Use only dishwasher detergent in the dishwasher—never liquid soap or sink detergent—to prevent oversudsing and resulting overflows.
• Operate the washing machine with a full load, but not an overload.
• Make sure the drain hoses of the washer and dryer are not clogged or kinked.
• Load dishes so that the detergent dispenser is not obstructed and racks are not too full for efficient operation.
• Load the clothes washer with a well-distributed load.

Weekly chores
• Clean the dishwasher sprayer and drainer. Remove food scraps.
• Discard spoiled food in the refrigerator.
• Wipe down the inside of the refrigerator.
• Clean the outside of the refrigerator, washer, dryer, and dishwasher.
• Go over the outside of the range with cleanser and sponge.
• Remove and clean range control knobs.
• Clean burners on the stove with steel wool, or if they're especially dirty, remove and soak them in a cleaning solution.
• Clean the lint screen in the clothes dryer and the lint trap in the washer.

Monthly tasks
• Clean the range thoroughly.
• Defrost the refrigerator to keep ice buildup under control and reduce strain on the motor. Do not use sharp instruments to chip away encrusted ice. Use a plastic scraper.
• Clean range hood vent filters; wash them in the dishwasher

or soak them in cleaning solution in the sink. Dry, then replace them.
• Clean the oven and broiler.
• Put a small bowl of fresh baking soda or crushed charcoal in the refrigerator to absorb food odors.
• Clean the dryer's vent hose and exterior vent.
• Clean the washer's lint trap. If you use the machine often, you may need to do this more frequently, even weekly.
• Clean the air gap, if any, in the built-in dishwasher.

Seasonal chores
• Check appliances for needed adjustments.
• Clean the refrigerator's condenser coils.
• Clean the drip pan under the refrigerator.

• Use appliance wax on exterior surfaces.
• Clean gas ports on the range burners.
• Clean under the vane of the washing machine.
• Clean the dryer's exterior vent.
• Check all electrical cords for damage. Replace them, if necessary, before they cause trouble.
• Check for a worn drum belt in the clothes dryer.
• Check for proper air and gas mixture in both gas burners and pilot lights. Adjust the air shutter on the gas line to give a clear blue flame.

Annual checkups
• Inspect for damaged parts, such as a roughened basket in the washer or worn gaskets on the washer, dryer, dishwasher, and refrigerator.
• Check for a worn grind ring on the garbage disposer and for worn motor bearings or flywheel.
• Check for worn gaskets, which could cause the garbage disposer to leak from the sides or bottom.
• Test the oven thermostat and adjust or replace it if it's inaccurate.

• Make sure the water heater is set to supply sufficiently hot water to the washer and dishwasher.
• Make sure all appliances are level. In a year's time, a leveler can vibrate out of place. Adjust as necessary.
• Keep house drains clean so washers can drain properly.
• Clean water intake valve screens in the clothes washer.
• Tighten any loose screws on trim and exterior panels.
• Clean the blower behind the clothes dryer; make sure the blower is firmly attached to the motor shaft.

Be prepared
It's useful to ask around among friends and neighbors for the names of appliance repairmen they have found to be reliable and prompt. You also can consult your appliance dealer for recommendations. Many manufacturers supply service through local representatives. Check your Yellow Pages if you purchased the appliance elsewhere.

Keep all owners' manuals and warranties for your appliances in a handy, accessible place. If you lose a manual, you can get another from the manufacturer.

When you call for service, be prepared to give the model number and year for the appliance, if possible, over the phone, to ensure that the service person brings the correct parts. And remember, for any repairs you undertake yourself, you must purchase and use replacement parts made for your particular make and model of appliance. The owner's manual can help you identify the parts needed.

With good care, you will rarely need any.

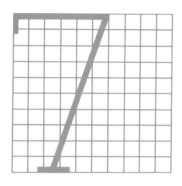

FURNISHINGS

Draperies, upholstery, wood furniture, and other home furnishings present a continuing maintenance challenge. You need to keep them clean; attend to spills, stains, and minor repairs; refresh them every spring or so; and occasionally come to the rescue of furnishings that need resuscitating. This chapter tells how to give your furnishings the kind of tender, loving care that will keep them well and with you for years to come.

ROUTINE CARE

Keep dust and soil from working into fibers by cleaning draperies weekly. Use a hand vacuum or the upholstery brush attachment of your regular vacuum cleaner.

Good-quality draperies typically last five or six years—longer if they're lined. Protecting and maintaining draperies extends their lives and keeps them looking fresh and new.

Sunlight is fabric's worst enemy. It fades dyes and weakens and rots fibers. Window glass magnifies the sun's destruction, even in winter.

Protect draperies by drawing shades during the day. Awnings offer even more protection and cut summer heat gain at south- and west-facing windows. Line draperies and use an interlining with fragile fabrics.

Rain or condensation on window glass can cause unsightly water stains on draperies. Sometimes these stains aren't noticeable until the draperies are cleaned, and by then the marks are almost impossible to remove. To prevent water stains, close windows against the elements, and hang draperies so they don't touch the glass.

Humidity can do more subtle damage. Fabrics absorb moisture and stretch or shrink a little. Excessive moisture, however, can cause more serious harm. Install exhaust fans to reduce humidity.

Fumes and impurities from furnaces, ovens, and cigarette smoke discolor fabrics. Minimize the damage with frequent vacuuming and regular washing or dry cleaning. Remove stains promptly.

To replace a worn cord in a traverse rod, remove the rod from its brackets. Notice how the old cord was strung and thread the new one the same way. Tie it to the master slides so the cord can tow the drapery along the rod.

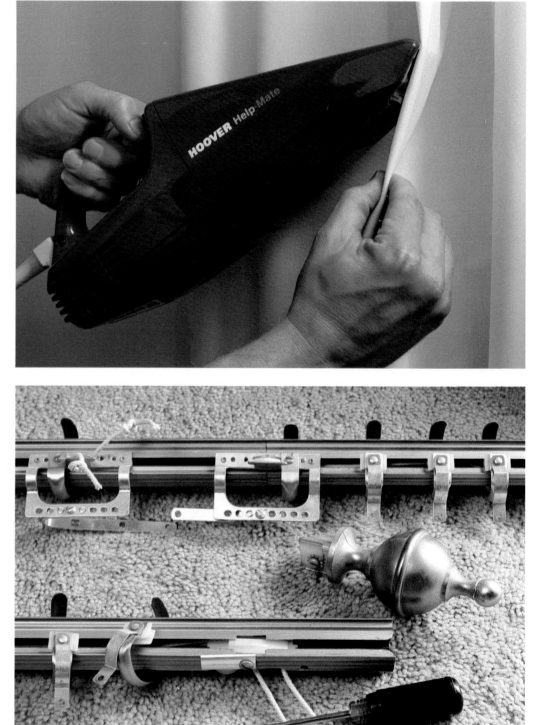

Simple tools and equipment that make routine cleaning easier include the old-fashioned feather duster and the lamb's-wool duster, which attracts minute particles of soil. An extension handle makes it easy to dust the tops of tall cabinets. Wipe up very fine dust with the same type of tack cloth used in refinishing wood furniture.

A vacuum cleaner can handle more than just carpets. Properly equipped, it cleans bare floors and dusts nooks, louvers, books, blinds, light fixtures, walls, molding, draperies, mattresses, and more. Make regular use of attachments, such as floor and upholstery tools, a soft brush for delicate fabrics and lampshades, and crevice tools that get into crannies.

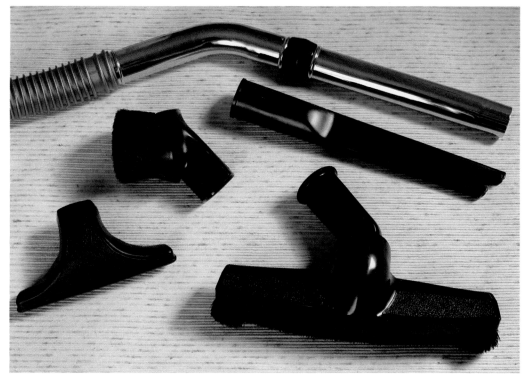

HIRING HELP FOR HOUSEWORK

Tired of the seemingly endless round of chores involved in keeping a house clean? Perhaps it's time to budget for professional help.

• *Free-lance cleaning help* comes to your house on a regular basis and dusts, vacuums, scrubs, scours, and polishes until it gleams. The best way to find good free-lance help is by word of mouth. A worker probably will want a verbal commitment for a certain number of work hours every week or two. You supply the cleaning equipment and supplies.

• *Maid services* advertise in the Yellow Pages and will dispatch a person or team to your house on almost any schedule you choose. You can even use a maid service only once—when you're moving into or out of a house, for example. Workers bring their own equipment and supplies and do routine cleaning.

• *Heavy cleaning* chores, such as washing walls, removing wax from floors, and washing windows, may require a janitorial firm or an upholstery- and rug-cleaning specialist.

Whichever option you choose, ask for references and check them. With services, workers should be bonded and insured against injury.

CARING FOR UPHOLSTERED FURNITURE

Use an upholstery brush and the crevice tool of your vacuum cleaner to remove dirt and dust from creases and seams in upholstery. Don't neglect areas around cording and buttons, where dust collects. Use a stain remover for quick spot cleaning.

Everyday wear and tear eventually claims the lives of most upholstered pieces, but you can prolong their comfortable years with a few protective measures.

• Keep upholstery away from direct sunlight, extreme humidity, and dust and heat from air registers.

• Vacuum weekly and keep fabrics dry. Turn loose cushions regularly to distribute wear.

• Look under seat cushions for "care and cleaning" labels and for information about fiber content.

• If spills occur, work fast to remove the spots before they soak in. Lift loose solids with a spatula; blot up liquids with a clean white cloth or a paper towel.

If water won't harm a fabric, sponge the area with a little cool water (hot water sets most stains). If this doesn't work, let the fabric dry thoroughly, then treat it with stain remover.

Always test any stain remover or overall cleaning agent on an inconspicuous area, and use only as much as necessary. Dampen a white cloth with cleaning solution and whisk it lightly over the stain, from the center to the outside, so the fabric absorbs the solution slowly. For more about removing stains, see page 112.

CLEANING LEATHER AND VINYL

Directions for leather care used to emphasize lubricating with a dressing of leather cream, saddle soap, or neat's-foot oil. These still are good for cleaning and preserving old leather.

New leathers, however, have special finishes that prevent drying and cracking. Oil treatments may damage them. Instead, regularly dust and periodically wash them with a mild oil soap and warm water. Never use dry-cleaning solvents or cleaners with ammonia, bleach, or abrasives on leather or vinyl upholstery.

Most normal spills won't stain leather, but shoe polish, ink, and lipstick can leave permanent marks unless cleaned quickly. Wipe spots with rubbing alcohol and rinse off immediately.

Clean vinyl with a damp cloth or, if the vinyl is heavily soiled, with a commercial spray cleaner. Remove stubborn stains with a paste of water and baking soda.

Spray-on protective chemical finishes help fabrics resist soiling and staining. Oil and water spills bead up, so you can blot them away. Remove any remaining stains with water or dry-cleaning solvent.

You may have to discard the old stuffing and substitute a new slab of polyurethane foam for a sagging loose cushion. Or, restore the old cushion with layers of polyester batting, glued with aerosol adhesive.

To repair a seam in upholstery, blindstitch it, using a curved upholsterer's needle. Buried beneath fabric, the thread won't show. Use fairly small stitches and pull them tight to draw the edges together.

Mend burns or gouges in vinyl upholstery with a vinyl repair kit. You spread on a compound, then touch it up with pigment. For a small tear, work a scrap of vinyl and adhesive under it. Seal edges with a heating tool.

CARING FOR WOOD FURNITURE

Use a liquid or spray cleaner-polish or a special wax cleaner on varnished or shellacked surfaces. Clean butcher block with lemon oil. Wash painted surfaces with a sponge dipped in detergent solution and wrung almost dry. Rinse and dry quickly.

Dust wood furniture frequently—daily if you can—to remove abrasive particles. Lift lamps and vases to dust underneath. Sliding objects around can scratch the surface.

Dust with the wood's grain, using a soft lint-free cloth sprayed with a small amount of furniture polish or with a dust-attracting product. Don't use a treated cloth on oil finishes, however.

Shield wood furniture from direct sunlight and from heat from a fireplace, radiator, or hot-air register. Furniture stays at its best in a steady temperature of 65 to 70 degrees Fahrenheit, with a humidity level of 50 percent. Too much humidity can cause warping, mildew, and stains; too little can shrink the wood, curl veneers, and loosen joints.

Treat stains in wood quickly, following directions in the table on page 113.

Retire a wobbly piece of furniture until you have time to repair it. If a chair has a loose rung, leg, or stretcher, another joint has to support the load, and the increased stress weakens the good joint. This, in turn, adds stress to still another good joint, until finally, the whole chair collapses.

Wood needs regular cleaning and polishing to retain its glow. Most furniture polishes clean, polish, and protect the surface. Apply sparingly and only when furniture loses its shine, not every time you dust.

Use a high-luster polish for a traditional bright gloss on walnut, mahogany, cherry, or beechwood. A medium-luster product is best for maple and rosewood, and a low-luster paste wax-cleaner for country styles in pine and oak. Don't wax oiled pieces at all.

CARING FOR OTHER MATERIALS

Take care when you clean trims and inserts, such as cane seats and leather, marble, or plastic tabletops. Some materials can be cleaned along with the wood, but others demand special treatment.

• *Cane and wicker.* Wash with mild detergent and warm water. Clean painted wicker with a damp cloth.

• *Rush.* Sponge gently with a little dry-cleaning fluid.

• *Laminated plastic.* Clean with detergent and water. Always rinse and dry thoroughly. Special commercial plastic cleaners add shine and leave an antistatic finish that repels dust and smudges. Wax to fill shallow scratches. Remove stubborn stains with a paste of baking soda and water.

• *Acrylic (Plexiglas or Lucite).* Wipe with a damp chamois. Wash with mild detergent and water. Rub away shallow scratches with paste wax. Sand deep ones with superfine sandpaper, then apply a coat of automobile paste wax.

• *Marble.* Wash with clear warm water and, once a year, with a mild detergent solution. Deep stains may require professional treatment.

• *Inlaid leather.* Clean old leather with saddle soap, newer leathers with warm water and vegetable oil soap or with a commercial leather cleaner.

A white ring usually is a surface stain caused by a dripping glass, spilled alcohol, or a hot dish. Rub with a paste of rottenstone and mineral oil. Wipe off immediately, and rub smooth with furniture polish or oil.

To repair a loose dowel joint in a chair, pull the joint apart and scrape out old glue. Apply fresh glue to both halves and fit the parts together. Tap the dowels home with a mallet, and clamp overnight.

REMOVING STAINS

UPHOLSTERY, SLIPCOVERS, AND DRAPERIES

CAUTION
Acetone (nail polish remover) and *alkalis,* such as washing soda, may damage acetate, polyester, and Dacron fibers. *Enzyme presoak products* will damage silk and wool. All *enzyme products* and *prewash sprays* must be washed or sponged out with water. Never leave products on fabric.

Follow these proportions for mixing spotting solutions. *Detergent solution:* 1 part liquid detergent to 8 parts water. *Bleaches:* 1 cup chlorine bleach to 1 gallon water; 1 tablespoon powdered oxygen bleach to 1 gallon water. *Vinegar-detergent solution:* ¼ cup water, ½ teaspoon liquid detergent, and 1 teaspoon vinegar. *Stain softeners:* ¼ cup dry-cleaning fluid to 1½ teaspoons glycerin or mineral oil.

ALCOHOL
Washable Fabrics: Spray with a prewash product. Wash. If a stain remains, soak in water and washing soda. Wash.
Upholstery and Nonwashable Fabrics: Sponge with club soda and blot dry. Sponge off and blot dry.

BLOOD
Washable Fabrics: Soak in cold water and detergent solution. Apply a paste of enzyme product, and wash. Flush a fresh stain with cold water.
Upholstery and Nonwashable Fabrics: Soften old stains with warm glycerin. Sponge with an enzyme product and water. Rinse and blot dry. Bleach with hydrogen peroxide, if necessary.

CANDLE WAX, CHEWING GUM
Washable Fabrics: Harden wax or gum with ice. Scrape off residue. Apply dry-cleaning solvent.
Upholstery and Nonwashable Fabrics: Use the same process.

FINGERNAIL POLISH
Washable Fabrics: Sponge with acetone (note caution) or cover for 30 minutes with a cloth dampened with dry-cleaning fluid and mineral oil. Rinse and wash.
Upholstery and Nonwashable Fabrics: Use the same process, but sponge off and blot dry, instead of washing.

FRUIT *(juices, berries)*
Washable Fabrics: Pour boiling water through the stain. If the fabric can't take boiling water, apply glycerin. Wash out. Use a prewash spray. Wash.
Upholstery and Nonwashable Fabrics: Sponge with cold water. Apply glycerin. Sponge off. Apply dry-cleaning fluid and blot dry.

GREASE
Washable Fabrics: Apply an enzyme product and wash. If a stain remains, soak for five hours in a detergent and baking soda solution. Wash.
Upholstery and Nonwashable Fabrics: Lift with an absorbent powder, such as cornstarch. Apply a dry-cleaning fluid, repeatedly if necessary.

INK
Washable Fabrics: Soften with warm glycerin, and wash. Cover for 30 minutes with a cloth soaked in dry-cleaning fluid and mineral oil solution. Sponge off and wash.
Upholstery and Nonwashable Fabrics: Use the same process, but sponge off and blot dry, instead of washing.

MILDEW
Washable Fabrics: If a fabric is colorfast, soak it in chlorine bleach and water solution. Then wash it in the hottest water safe for the fabric.
Upholstery and Nonwashable Fabrics: If chlorine is safe, apply a few drops of bleach and water solution. Wipe off in two minutes with a damp cloth. Neutralize by sponging with vinegar. Rinse and blot dry.

PAINT
Washable Fabrics: Oil-base: Sponge with paint remover and wash, then with dry-cleaning fluid. Wash. *Water-base:* Soften with warm glycerin, and wash.
Upholstery and Nonwashable Fabrics: Oil-base: Same as for washable fabric, but sponge off and blot dry.
Water-base: Soften with glycerin; blot dry. Sponge with equal parts of ammonia and water. Rinse; blot dry.

PET STAINS
Washable Fabrics: Remove solids and absorb liquid with baking soda. Soak in water and enzyme product. Wash.
Upholstery and Nonwashable Fabrics: Dab on clear water, then full-strength ammonia, then a few drops of vinegar. Leave vinegar on for five minutes. Rinse and blot dry.

SOFT DRINKS
Washable Fabrics: Soak in water and enzyme product. Wash, adding 1 cup of white vinegar to the final rinse.
Upholstery and Nonwashable Fabrics: Keep damp for 30 minutes with a cloth dipped in vinegar and water solution. Sponge off and blot dry.

VOMIT
Washable Fabrics: Remove solids. Soak in water and enzyme solution. Wash, adding ½ cup of ammonia.
Upholstery and Nonwashable Fabrics: Apply a paste of enzyme product and water. Brush off and sponge with warm detergent and ammonia mixture. Rinse. Blot dry. If a stain remains, sponge with alcohol. Blot dry.

WOOD FURNITURE

CAUTION
The stain-spotting methods recommended here apply only for varnish, shellac, and oil finishes.

Lacquer finishes require special treatment, described on page 115.

BLACK SPOTS
Light Stains: Black spots, caused by moisture that has penetrated the wood, are serious damage and are hard to remove. Try bleaching with hydrogen peroxide.
Deeper Damage: If bleaching doesn't work, remove the finish, scrape out the area, and fill it with shellac or a wax stick. Sand smooth and touch up with matching stain. Refinish.

BURNS
Light Stains: Bleach out a light scorch mark with hydrogen peroxide. Rub with a light abrasive, and polish.
Deeper Damage: If the burn is deep, scrape out charred material and treat as directed for black spots.

CANDLE WAX or GUM
Light Stains: Harden wax or gum with ice. Scrape the residue away with an old credit card, and rub with a cloth dampened in mineral spirits.
Deeper Damage: Treatment is the same as for light stains. When marks are removed, rub the area with liquid polish and wipe dry.

CLOUDINESS *(blush)*
Light Stains: A light haze usually is on the surface, caused by moisture in the air. Clean with lemon oil and rewax or polish.

Deeper Damage: Rub stubborn cloudiness with fine steel wool dipped in pumice and mineral oil. Wipe off, and rewax or rub with furniture polish.

GREASE
Light Stains: Rub lightly with a cloth dipped in turpentine until all traces are removed.
Deeper Damage: Rub lightly with a cloth dampened in a solution of 1 tablespoon trisodium phosphate and 1 quart water. Wipe clean with a damp cloth and dry.

INK
Light Stains: Rub with a paste of lemon juice and salt. Rinse thoroughly and polish.
Deeper Damage: If ink has penetrated the wood, it is almost impossible to lift out the stain. Treat as you would a black spot.

NAIL POLISH
Light Stains: Treat as you would dried paint, or rub with acetone.
Deeper Damage: Treat as you would dried paint, or rub with acetone. Refinish the smudged area.

PAINT
Light Stains: If paint is still damp, rub alkyd paint away with fine steel wool dipped in liquid wax. Wipe water-base paint with a damp cloth.
Deeper Damage: For dried alkyd and water-base paint, apply a paste of rottenstone and mineral oil to soften the stain. Let it set for a few minutes and wipe away. If necessary, rub with fine steel wool dipped in pumice and oil. Wipe off and dry.

SCRATCHES
Light Stains: Rub varnish or shellac finish with a nutmeat or shoe polish. Apply mineral oil for an oil-base finish.
Deeper Damage: Fill a deep scratch with shellac or wax stick. Wax is easier, but shellac is more durable. Scrape off dried filler, sand smooth, and touch up with artist's paint. Seal with varnish or rub with oil.

WHITE SPOTS *(or rings)*
Light Stains: Rub with rottenstone mixed with mineral oil. Wipe off immediately. Smooth the scuffed area with polish or oil.
Deeper Damage: Rub a stubborn white mark with fine steel wool dipped in a paste of pumice and oil. If this doesn't work, stroke with a pad dampened with dry-cleaning solvent. Apply polish or rub with oil.

KEEPING FURNISHINGS LOOKING NEW

Eventually, routine cleaning and quick first-aid treatments may not be enough to keep furnishings fresh. Then, you may need to thoroughly clean or renovate a piece to restore its youth and beauty. These recommendations will help.

Cleaning upholstered furniture

Furniture that gets the hardest use is the most vulnerable to stains and overall soiling. Despite regular care, upholstered pieces lose their brightness and begin to look slightly gray, perhaps even a little streaked where you've spot cleaned. Dust and grime have taken up residence in the fabric, and only deep cleaning can flush them out.

Cleaning upholstered furniture is fairly straightforward unless you have excessive oil, unusual stains, fragile fabrics, or fabrics that tend to shrink or color bleed. For these cases, call in a professional upholstery-cleaning service.

First, check the manufacturer's label to see if the fabric is washable or must be dry-cleaned. Always test any cleaning solution on an inconspicuous spot.

Vacuum the upholstery thoroughly. Don't remove zippered cushion covers for washing separately. Clean them in place so they won't shrink or stretch out of alignment.

If the fabric can be cleaned with a water-base solution, use a commercial shampoo. If you rent a carpet-cleaning machine with an attachment for upholstery, the manufacturer will recommend a specific cleaning product for use with the machine. (For more about cleaning machines, see pages 60 and 61.)

You also can mix up a good and inexpensive shampooing solution with a gallon of lukewarm water, a tablespoon of white powdered laundry detergent, and a teaspoon of white vinegar. Whip a small amount of the solution at a time into a stiff foam with an electric hand mixer.

Scrub on the foam (not the water) with a soft-bristled nylon brush, doing about a square foot at a time. Now scrub the adjacent area, overlapping slightly and using more foam as needed.

Lift off dirty suds with a spatula, and then sponge with a cloth wrung out of clear water. Let the fabric dry, and vacuum to raise its nap.

If the fabric is not waterproof, sponge with dry-cleaning fluid in the same way. Apply solvent sparingly and wipe it off before it soaks in and damages the filling.

Most upholstery fabrics now are treated at the factory with soil- and stain-repelling finishes. Generally, a fabric can be shampooed or dry-cleaned two or three times before the finish has to be renewed.

Reupholstering

There comes a time in the life of any upholstered furniture when no amount of cleaning will restore its vitality. Fabrics fade, springs sag, cushions go lumpy or limp. If you have a favorite sofa or chair grown woebegone with age, consider reupholstering.

A good-quality upholsterer strips furniture down to the frame, makes any necessary repairs, reties or replaces springs and other support systems, then builds up fresh padding and recovers everything with your choice of new fabric. You get what amounts to a new piece of furniture that just happens to be the same shape as the old one.

Good reupholstering doesn't come cheap. Fabrics can be costly, and the job calls for lots of skilled handwork. In some instances, you might be dollars ahead to buy a comparable new piece. If, however, you have a piece with intrinsic value, or one you simply can't bear to part with, by all means call in an upholsterer and get a bid.

Cleaning draperies, curtains, and slipcovers

Most glass curtains and many draperies made of synthetic materials can be washed at home. However, heavy lined draperies of silk, velvet, wool, linen, or cotton seldom can be cleaned satisfactorily except by experts. Check labels for cleaning instructions and chemical finishes, and alert the cleaner about them.

Many slipcovers can be hand washed in cold water and line dried. Replace laundered slipcovers while they're still slightly damp; this prevents shrinkage and lets the fabric shape to the furniture. Touch up with a warm iron.

Canvas covers should not be dry-cleaned, because solvents could dissolve the dyes. Polyester canvas can be machine washed; cotton and acrylic call for hand washing.

Cleaning wood furniture

Before you attempt to renovate wood furniture, identify the finish. Different finishes call for different cleaning techniques.

Use these tests. Rub a little oil on an inconspicuous spot. If it soaks in, the finish is oil. If it doesn't, moisten one spot with rubbing alcohol and another with lacquer thinner. If the alcohol spot softens, the finish is shellac. If the spot under the lacquer thinner softens, the finish is traditional lacquer. New factory-applied lacquers (polyester or acrylic resins) may not be affected. If none of these treatments changes the finish, it is varnish.

Now it's time to give the furniture a thorough cleaning. Sometimes removing built-up soil, old polish, and wax may be all that's needed.
• Clean varnish or shellac with mineral spirits, an oil finish with turpentine and linseed oil.
• Wash painted furniture.
• Water damages traditional lacquer (used on older furniture), so clean light soil with a little dry-cleaning fluid. To remove a dull film, rub on a paste of olive oil and flour. Wipe off and polish.
• Factory-applied synthetic lacquer finishes are easy to clean with warm water and a little ammonia.

Reconditioning a finish

If grime has built up over a long period, or if the surface is badly stained or crazed (crisscrossed with hairline cracks), stronger treatment is necessary. Reconditioning, rather than completely refinishing, may be the answer.

Several commercial products are designed for reconditioning old varnish, shellac, and lacquer. Sold in paint departments and labeled "refinishers," not "strippers" or "removers," these products remove not only old wax, polish, and dirt, but also the top layers of finish. They then liquefy the remaining clean finish, so it melts into small cracks and scratches, then hardens to a smooth surface. The original wood filler, sealer, and stain are left intact. Refinishers are not strong enough to work on paint or polyurethane varnish and will damage an oil finish.

Complete refinishing

If damage is extensive and extends below the finish, you will have to strip furniture to bare wood and refinish.

After removing knobs and drawer pulls, flow on a good-quality stripper, following label instructions. Let chemicals do the work of loosening the old finish for at least 15 minutes.

Scrape away the residue and wash the surface with lukewarm water, rubbed on with a pad of steel wool. Remove any pigment left in the pores with a wood bleach, then sand and resand until you have a mirror-smooth finish.

Now give the furniture a final sanding. For this, dampen the surface with a sponge to raise the grain. Let it dry and sand with fine-grit paper to achieve a silky smooth surface.

Vacuum up grit as you go and remove fine dust with a tack rag. Apply a stain to achieve the effect you want, then a filler and sealer.

Apply two or three successive coats of finish, sanding and dusting with a tack cloth in between. When the final coat is dry, wax the surface (except an oil finish) lightly with paste wax.

The choice of finish depends on the look you want and the type of wear the furniture will receive.
• *Shellac* is economical and easy to apply, but has little resistance to water and alcohol.
• *Lacquer* is a clear rich finish, but must be brushed or sprayed on expertly because it dries very quickly.
• *Penetrating oil*, a traditional finish, is easy to apply, but not highly durable; it is easy to repair, though.
• *Varnish* probably is the best clear finish for strength, durability, and water- and heat-resistance. Polyurethanes are especially durable.

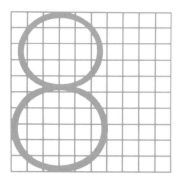

8

SYSTEMS

Once servants tended fires that kept a home warm, carried water for our ancestors' baths, and replaced candles as they burned out. Today's servants are machines and are largely unseen. Tucked into utility rooms, inside walls, and under floors, they're all too easy to neglect. This chapter tells how to keep your home's heating, cooling, plumbing, and wiring systems at your service.

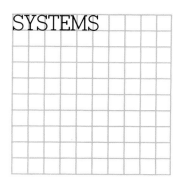
HEATING AND COOLING EQUIPMENT

Check filters monthly for dust, which can reduce the efficiency of a furnace and central air-conditioning system. Slide out the filter and hold it up to a strong light. If it's clogged, replace it.

Gone is the era when homeowners had to shovel coal several times every day. Today's heating and cooling machinery all but tends itself. You need only lend a helping hand now and then.

Pick a day in late spring to check over an air conditioner, another in early fall for the heating system, water heater, and controls. The photographs here and on pages 120–123 show what to look for. Have a professional service your furnace and/or central air conditioner at least every other year. A good mechanic can keep everything running at peak efficiency, and spot and correct any potential safety hazards.

Oil- and gas-fired furnaces, water heaters, and boilers deserve special safety attention. Only rarely do today's units blow up or catch fire, but a defective flue can leak deadly carbon monoxide into your home. If members of your family begin to complain of headaches, faintness, or nausea, check flues right away.

First, with a strong light, inspect pipes that run from the furnace and/or water heater to the chimney. Can you see any dents, loose or open joints, or spots that have rusted through? If so, replace the pipes at once. If the flue pipes pass muster, and you still suspect carbon monoxide, check for a blocked chimney. Clearing it is a job for a chimney cleaning service. *(continued)*

Blowers for air-moving systems are belt-driven. To operate smoothly, the belt needs about one inch of play, measured midway between the motor and fan pulleys. To adjust, loosen the motor-mount bolt, move the motor, and retighten.

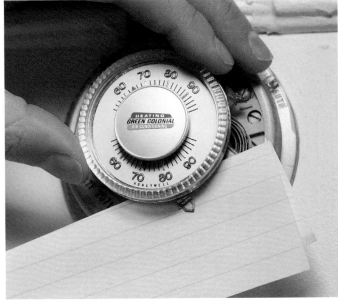

Every spring remove the cover from your air conditioner's condenser/compressor and flush out the condenser coils with water. Debris that collects on the copper tubing reduces cooling efficiency.

Electrical contacts inside most older thermostats tend to attract dust. Snap off the cover and clean them by rubbing an index card or dollar bill through them. Also blow or brush away dust on other parts.

A bare sheet metal duct running through an attic or an uninsulated basement loses heating and cooling energy. To conserve it, wrap the duct with foil-covered insulation. Foil slows the flow of radiant heat; insulation holds convected heat. Seal the seams with duct tape.

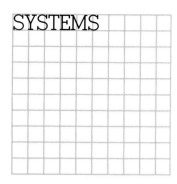

HEATING AND COOLING EQUIPMENT
(continued)

Pilot out on your water heater or furnace? First sniff for gas. If you smell any, call for service. If not, turn the gas cock to "pilot," light a match, press the red reset button, and ignite the pilot. Let it burn for 30 seconds or so, then turn the cock to "on."

To keep your home's comfort systems at their best, it helps to understand how they work. Begin by realizing that, to an engineer, "cold" does not exist. Rather, when we feel cold, it's because the air around us doesn't contain enough heat.

Now that we've dispensed with the notion of cold, let's look at the nature of heat. Just as water "wants" to always flow downhill, heat has an inherent tendency to move from a warmer space or object to a cooler one. In a water heater, for example, heat from the burner or electrical elements flows to the water in the tank.

Different types of heating systems distribute heat in different ways. Here's a brief summary.

• *Warm-air systems* heat air in a furnace, then push it through ducts to registers in living areas. There the air circulates, gives up its heat, then falls back to the furnace via one or more return ducts.

• *Hot water, steam, and electric baseboard systems* deliver heat by creating convective air currents. Heat carried to metal fins or cast-iron radiators warms air above the units. As this rises, it pushes cooler air to the floor, where it flows into the bottom of the unit and is warmed. Think of this convective loop of air entering your radiators or baseboards from the bottom and exiting from

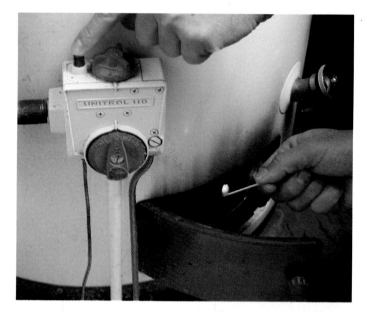

Have a room that's too cold? You may be able to warm it up by robbing heat from another room. Buy two or more inexpensive thermometers and gang them in one spot to be sure all show the same temperature. With masking tape, attach one thermometer to the wall about three feet above the floor and three feet to the right or left of the chilly register. Do the same at one or more other registers on the same duct run. Open the chilly register wide and damper the others slightly, wait 30 minutes, and check the thermometers. You may need to repeat the procedure several times. If you're unable to even up temperatures with register dampers, the entire system may need balancing, a job for a professional. Because cool air behaves differently, registers also may need adjusting in summer.

the top and you can see why blocking one with furniture or draperies would impair heating efficiency.

• *Radiant systems* have piping or wiring embedded in panels, ceilings, or floors. From these heat flows directly from the source to people and objects in the room.

Cooling systems

Heating systems put heat into your house; cooling systems take it out. Almost all residential cooling systems—room-size or central—are air movers. Moist, warm indoor air is pulled into the unit and passed over an evaporator coil charged with cold liquid refrigerant. The air gives off its heat and moisture to the coils, then a fan pushes the cooled air back into the room.

What happens to the heat an air conditioner extracts from your house? It's pumped outside, along with the refrigerant, which is now in a gaseous state. Outdoors, a compressor and condenser convert the refrigerant back to a liquid, causing it to get rid of the heat it absorbed inside.

• *Heat pumps* are simply reversible air conditioners. In the summer they remove heat from your house and dump it outside; in the winter they absorb heat from outside (even at low temperatures, there's *some* heat out there) and bring it indoors.   *(continued)*

Dust that collects inside hot water and electric baseboard registers cuts down on their heating efficiency and puts smudges on the wall above them. Remove each register's cover and loosen dust between the fins with a clean paintbrush. Finish by vacuuming up loose dust.

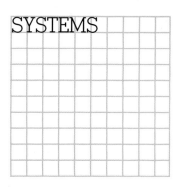
HEATING AND COOLING EQUIPMENT
(continued)

Forced-air furnaces are relatively simple devices, trouble-free and easy to understand and tend to. Steam and hot water boilers are a different matter. Though as reliable as furnaces, boilers are more complex, and certain maintenance chores call for a trained mechanic. If your home is heated by steam or hot water, schedule its heating plant for a professional going-over once a year, preferably in the spring. In between times, there are a few jobs you can do and problems you can diagnose yourself. First, consider how each system works.

Steam systems

Steam heating systems breathe air in and out with each cycle, which accounts for the familiar hissing sound steam radiators make. As steam rises, it forces air out through a vent at one end of the radiator.

The boiler itself needs air, which is why it's necessary to maintain the water level at about half full. Air space above the water is where steam builds up. A "gauge glass" on the side of a steam boiler tells you how much water and air are inside. Adjust the water level by opening valves that feed or drain water from the boiler. Some steam boilers have automatic feed valves.

Hot water systems

The main difference between steam and hot water heating is that hot water systems *don't* breathe. Instead, a predetermined amount of air is sealed into the system, usually in an "expansion tank" like the one on the wall in the photograph *opposite*. The expansion tank should be about half full of water, with a diaphragm between air and water.

Air pressure in the tank allows the boiler to superheat the water without turning it to steam. You monitor the air and water in the system with a "combination gauge" on the side of the boiler. It has two pointers. One remains stationary at the start-up pressure—usually 12 pounds per square inch. The other swings up during a firing, then drops back to match the stationary pointer when the system cools.

If the moving arrow drops below the fixed marker, the system either needs water or has too much air. If the arrow stops above the fixed pointer, the expansion tank needs air. Check the combination gauge every few weeks during the heating season.

Radiation units

Troubled by a radiator or baseboard convector that won't heat up properly, or knocks and bangs when the heat comes up? Most likely either air or water is trapped inside. With a steam unit, check the air vent. You should be able to feel air coming out as steam enters. If not, try clearing the vent with a pin; if that doesn't work, replace the vent.

Vents on hot water units are normally closed. When a radiator won't heat, it's probably partially filled with air. Bleed this off by opening the vent with a screwdriver or special key. Leave the vent open until the hissing stops and water begins to flow out.

Radiation units that bang usually aren't pitched properly. If you have hot water heat or a steam radiator connected to pipes at each end, the unit should slope toward the end opposite the inlet valve so gravity will carry water back to the boiler. Pitch a steam unit with only one pipe toward the inlet valve.

Procedures for adjusting the ratio of air to water in a hot water expansion tank vary. With this one, turn a valve on top of the tank. Remove the valve's wheel from its stem so no one can inadvertently operate it.

Every boiler has a drain-cock to empty the system and flush out rust and sediment. Run a hose to a drain that's lower than the cock. With a water system, also open bleeder vents on the radiation units.

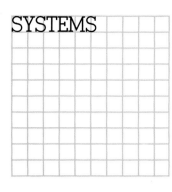

TROUBLE-SHOOTING HEATING AND COOLING SYSTEMS

FORCED-AIR SYSTEMS

PROBLEM	CAUSES	SOLUTIONS
No heat.	Thermostat set too low. Circuit breaker or furnace switch open; fuse blown. Gas pilot out. Oil furnace motor overheated. Fuse or breaker block out on electric furnace.	Raise thermostat at least five degrees. Check for electrical problem; then throw breaker, replace fuse, or reset furnace switch. If it goes out again, call a professional. Relight gas pilot (page 120). Add oil to oil-burner motor, as recommended by manufacturer. Restart motor.
No cool air.	If blower runs, system probably is out of refrigerant, has clogged filter, or has debris blocking condensing unit outdoors. If system is silent, thermostat may be set too high, or electrical system may be faulty.	Recharging air-conditioning lines with refrigerant requires a service call. Change a dirty filter; hose out debris from condensing unit (page 119). Lower the thermostat five degrees. Check for an electrical overload or short, reset the breaker, or change the fuse. If an electrical problem recurs, call for service.
System cycles on and off too often.	Filter is clogged, blower is malfunctioning, or thermostat is sending false signals. Causes are the same for both heating and cooling.	Check filter and change if needed. Examine blower motor for slow response and blower fan for scraping, sticking, or off-center rotation. Clean thermostat contacts (page 119); call for service if that fails to work.
Uneven distribution of heating, cooling.	Airflow out of balance.	Try to balance system by adjusting register dampers (page 120). If this doesn't work, have contractor rebalance ducts.
Excessive furnace noise.	Squealing may be fan belt slippage, dry bearings on oil burner, or dry motor. Rumbling happens when gas pilot needs adjusting or burners are dirty. Ducts rattle when blower speed is too high.	Tighten fan belt (page 118). Oil bearings. Add oil to motor cups for oil burner, as manufacturer advises. Adjust pilot flame until it's mostly blue, with a yellow tip. Call service to clean burners. Lower fan speed if the blower is variable; otherwise call for service.
Frequent heat pump defrost cycles.	Ice is blocking outdoor coil.	Ice may be collecting on leaves, seeds, and other matter jammed into coils. Clean by hosing (page 119). If coils are clear, unit may have faulty reversing valve. Flip selector switch to "emergency heat" and call a professional.

WATER AND STEAM SYSTEMS

PROBLEM	CAUSES	SOLUTIONS
No heat.	Main switch off, circuit breaker out, or fuse blown. Too little water in system. Burner malfunction.	Examine for any obvious electrical problem, then try main boiler switch, throw breakers, or change fuse. Still a problem? Call for service. Water shortage may result from return-line leaks; check them first, then add water. Cleaning and/or adjusting burners is a job for a contractor.
Too little heat.	Thermostat is set too low. Rust and scale inside boiler are making water or steam distribution sluggish. Built-up soot has dampening effect on burners. In hot water system, too little or too much water can affect flow of heat.	Raise thermostat five degrees. Flush out rust and sediment. Call service to have burners cleaned and adjusted. Check hot water boiler's combination gauge to assess whether expansion tank is working properly and add water or air as needed (page 122).
Only some radiators, convectors heat up.	Air trapped in room units impedes flow of hot water; same for steam if air vent is clogged. Zone valve may be faulty if all units in zone are cold and piping up to valve is very hot. Zones may be improperly balanced.	Bleed air from unit's vent until hot water shows, then close vent. Clean opening of steam air vent with slim wire; if that fails, replace vent. To clean or replace zone valve, shut off system and drain back water. Balancing zones may require professional assistance.
Noisy pipes.	Improperly pitched return lines or coupling between circulator motor and pump may be broken.	All return lines must be pitched toward boiler; check them with spirit level; shim any that aren't. Replacing a coupling is a job for a pro.
Chronic need to refill boiler.	Most likely system has leak: in return lines, pressure relief valve, circulator, or tank.	Search for source of leak. If it's in piping, wrap with plastic tape or a rubber strip held by auto hose clamp until pipe is replaced (page 128). Water spurting from relief valve signals too high a head of steam or excessive air pressure in hot water system. If circulator leaks, seal probably is broken, a repair job for a professional. A leaking tank may have to be replaced.
Steam gauge glass cloudy.	Usually means boiler needs flushing, but may mean scum inside glass.	Flush boiler (page 122). If water runs clear, loosen nuts holding gauge glass, lift out, and clean with baby bottle brush.

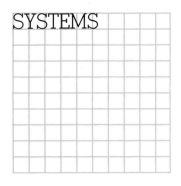
PLUMBING AND WIRING

If your home has a sump pump, periodically remove the grille covering the sump and check for debris inside. If a pump malfunctions, you can get by temporarily with an emergency unit powered by an electric drill.

If water and electricity are a home's lifelines, plumbing and wiring are its arteries and veins. Neither of these vital systems demands much regular maintenance, but many plumbing and wiring problems—a burst pipe, for example, or a blown fuse—require immediate attention.

When you're confronted with a plumbing or electrical emergency, first shut down the system, then find and correct the problem or call for help. Here are the most common plumbing and wiring problems and what to do about them.

• *A burst pipe* can spill a lot of water in almost no time. To minimize potential damage, acquaint yourself and other members of the household with the location and operation of your home's main water shutoff. This critical valve is almost always located at the point where water enters your home. You can temporarily tape a dripping pipe, as shown on page 128. Replace a completely ruptured pipe before you turn the water back on.

• *A frozen pipe* will burst unless you take immediate steps to thaw it. Apply heat with any warming device on hand—a heating pad or hair dryer, for example. Wrap pipes that chronically freeze with electrical heat tape. For more about thawing pipes, see page 128.

• *Clear a clogged drain* by first plunging with a force cup. If this doesn't work, try working a drain auger through the blockage. If you need professional help, call a drain cleaning company, not a plumber. Drain specialists usually react faster and charge less.

• *When a fuse blows or a circuit breaker trips,* either the circuit is overloaded, or one of its "customers" is causing a short. First, shut off or unplug the last electrical device that

was operated prior to the outage and try to restore power. If it goes out again, turn off or disconnect *every* device on the circuit and try them one by one until you find the culprit. If your home has fuses and the problem seems to be caused by momentary surging when a motor kicks in, consider replacing the fuse with a time-delay type. These are designed to handle momentary overloads. *(continued)*

In early autumn, shut off valves that control the flow of water to outside hose bibs. Then, open the cock at the bottom of each valve to drain water in the line. Open the hose bib, too.

Circuit breakers are easy to shut off and reset. Simply flip a switch or push a button. If your service entrance has fuses, keep a supply nearby. Never replace a fuse with one rated at a higher amperage.

To replace a worn-out switch or receptacle, shut off power to the circuit. Remove the faceplate, pull out the device, and loosen screws holding the wires. The package explains how to install a new device.

DOES YOUR HOME HAVE ADEQUATE POWER?

When electrical overloads continue to knock out your favorite television program or shut down the washing machine, your home may be underpowered, or you may simply need to move a big electricity-eater from one circuit to another that's less heavily used.

To assess just how much house power you have, take a trip to the service panel and examine the rating on the main breaker or fuse. Most homes built before World War II had only 30 to 60 amps of power—woefully inadequate today. In the 1950s and '60s, 100 amps met most electrical needs. Today most new homes feature 150- or 200-amp service.

Power to raise the amperage coming into your house lies waiting in the utility lines. To tap more of it, hire an electrician to install a new service panel. Be sure the new panel includes several blank slots for future expansion.

If power at the panel seems adequate, consider reshuffling the load so that big users draw power from different circuits. Some, such as electric irons, are portable enough to plug in elsewhere. Big appliances may be able to reach another circuit via a heavy-duty extension cord, but don't try to travel more than another six feet or so. And never run an extension cord through a wall; electrical codes forbid it.

Better than an extension cord is an entirely new circuit. Unless you're very knowledgeable about electrical codes and procedures, this is a job for a professional electrician.

WHEN POWER FAILS

If power failures are frequent in your area, the best defense is a standby generator. A 500-watt plant can run the basics—a furnace, freezer, and a few lights.

If a generator doesn't make sense for you, prepare for a blackout by purchasing a battery-powered lantern, a couple of flashlights, and a portable radio.

During a winter power outage, conserve house heat by covering north-facing windows with blankets and not opening doors any more than absolutely necessary. If it seems that the outage might be protracted and house heat is dropping rapidly, drain the plumbing, as explained on page 128.

After a power failure in any season, turn off all electrical devices except a few lights to signal when electricity has returned. Major surging that happens when a utility gets back in operation could burn out motors in your house.

If you're dependent upon an electric pump, heed storm warnings and fill bottles and pails with water.

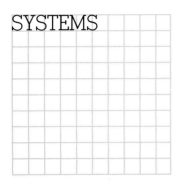

PLUMBING AND WIRING
(continued)

Pipes that penetrate outside walls can freeze. If there's nothing flammable nearby, quick-thaw a frozen pipe with the flame from a propane torch. To prevent future freeze-ups, wrap the pipe with heat cable.

Losing water from a pipe leak? Temporarily bandage with plastic electrical tape or duct tape, as shown here. Leaks in galvanized pipes like this one usually mean that the entire system will soon need replacing.

Pipes that seem to leak may be merely sweating. The cure: Wrap them with adhesive-backed foam insu- lation. This insulation also can conserve energy when hot water pipes run through unheated areas.

WINTERIZING PLUMBING

If you occupy your home year-round, the only fall plumbing maintenance you need to do is to drain hose bibs (as explained on page 126) and any outdoor piping. If you winter in a sunny climate and leave your principal residence empty, or own a summer home in a cold-winter state, you'll need to prevent pipes from freezing and bursting by draining the entire system. Here's how to proceed.
• Flush toilets one at a time and as each tank fills, add antifreeze. Shut off water to the toilet and flush a second time, leaving a mix of antifreeze and water in the toilet's trap.
• Close the valve where water enters the house.
• Starting at the house's highest point, open all faucets from attic to basement.
• Drain the water heater.
• Remove cleanout plugs from all traps you can reach and drain the traps into a bucket. Replace the plugs and fill the traps with an antifreeze and water mixture that's right for your winter weather.
• Pour antifreeze full-strength into all drains leading to traps you can't reach, including the main system trap in the line leading away from the house.

When you start the water system again, the antifreeze will flush away, harmlessly diluted by the water.

Some newer meters have digital readouts, but most still show four dials. Generally, utilities send out a meter-reader monthly, but some ask you to mark a card, like the one shown below. Reading from left to right, the dials represent kilowatt-hours in multiples of 10,000, 1,000, 100, and 10. When the pointer falls between two numbers, read the lower of the two. If it falls on a number, read the next lower number only if the pointer on the next dial to the right has not passed zero. The meter shown here reads 92,660 kwh.

For many homeowners the electric bill is a monthly mystery. About the only number that makes any sense is the amount you owe. Understanding a few basics of electrical terminology, and how utilities price electricity, just may help you reduce that bottom line.

The four words you need to know are *watts, amps, volts,* and *kilowatt-hours. Watt* is electrical power. When you switch on a 100-watt light bulb,

you're looking at the power expressed in light by 100 watts. The same bulb will flicker at one watt, but just barely. When you turn down the dial of a dimmer, you can see the drop in power, or wattage.

Amps or *amperes* applies to the rate at which electrons flow through a circuit. How do they flow? They are pushed by *volts,* which represent electrical pressure. Voltage remains constant, about 125.

Amps times volts equals watts and everything electrical in your house can be rated in watts. Adding up all of them would result in a huge, unwieldy number, so the total amount of electrical power used in a household is expressed by the *kilowatt,* or 1,000 watts.

How much power you're using, however, is no help in figuring your bill. The power company must bill for the amount of electrical *energy*

you've used. Energy is power multiplied by time, or *kilowatt-hours,* generally expressed as *kwh.* The utility rate is based on so much per *kwh.*

The price you're paying per kwh may be higher in summer than in winter and the utility may periodically factor in certain "adjustments" based on its costs for fuel and other items, so the best way to keep watch over electrical consumption is to compare kwh readings, not dollar amounts.

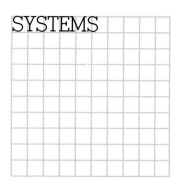

SETTING UP A SYSTEMS MAINTENANCE AGENDA

Most of us lead busy lives, which can make it easy to put off looking after systems that seem to be working just fine. That's one good reason for making appointments with yourself for tending to the simple chores outlined in this chapter.

At the beginning of each year, while your calendar is still mostly blank, pencil in weeks or weekends when you intend to look after your home's systems. The chart at right offers a starting point that you can copy or adapt to suit your needs. Combine it with other charts in this book or stagger your maintenance agendas so that you devote part of one Saturday to systems, another to exterior matters, and so forth.

In case you're wondering whether deferring maintenance is really as pound-foolish as we've been saying throughout this book, consider this example: Two midwestern homeowners bought virtually identical houses, with identical air-conditioning systems, in the same year. One owner paid absolutely no attention to the system. The other changed filters and cleaned the condensing unit yearly, at a cost of less than $5.

After less than seven years, the untouched system expired and had to be replaced—at a cost of about $2,000. After 12 years, the second, well-maintained cooling system was still going strong. Its owner's total maintenance outlay? Less than $100.

A SYSTEMS MAINTENANCE CHECKLIST

SYSTEM	PROBABILITY OF BREAKDOWN	WHAT TO CHECK
ELECTRICAL	Medium to high for old wiring; low for new wiring, until new appliances overload system.	List every device on each circuit, plus its draw in amperage (amps = watts ÷ volts). Before buying a house older than 25 years, have wiring checked. Watch for sluggish switches and worn-out receptacles.
PLUMBING	In hard-water areas without water softener, medium to high for metal piping. Medium for system at least 20 years old. High if steps aren't taken to winterize untended piping.	A gradual decline in water pressure. Wet pipe joints; leaks. Faucets for dripping, drains for clogging, toilets for inadequate flushing. Pipe "hammer."
HEATING **Forced Air**	Low for breakdowns, but as years pass, system efficiency declines. High for poor delivery of heat if system is never checked.	Filter for dirt; motor and blower for smooth delivery; balanced heat delivery. Invest in biennial service check.
Hot Water	Low for breakdown. Medium for air-locked lines if equipment is 10 or more years old. Low to medium for older expansion tanks.	Even delivery of heat. Boiler water for rust, scale. Air blocks in nonfunctioning radiator/convectors. Invest in annual service check.
Steam	Low to medium, because most systems are in older houses, and aging.	Even delivery of heat. Boiler water for rust, scale. Water blocking in dead-level return line. Get annual service check.
COOLING **Central Air-Conditioning**	Low to medium for system older than 10 years. Medium for uneven delivery of cool air for untended system.	Filter for dirt; motor and blower for smooth operation. Uneven delivery of cool air. Dirt, leaves caught in outdoor coils. Pay for annual service call.
Heat Pump	Low for breakdown. Medium to high for inoperative heating cycle in consistent below-15-degree temperatures.	Same as for central air-conditioning.

MAINTENANCE	SUGGESTED TIME OF YEAR	APPROXIMATE COST
Raise amperage at service entry if you're plagued with overloads. Immediately replace short-prone wiring. Update old switches; to save energy consider installing dimmers.	Autumn in north, spring in south, to catch period of maximum use.	Low to medium for raising amperage or extending circuits. Medium to high for replacing house wiring. Low to replace a switch or receptacle.
Replace lime-clogged piping; consider installing softener. Replace leaking pipes. New washer or cartridge for leaking faucet; snake out clogged drain; possible new float, stopper for toilet. Air chamber for "hammer." Insulate cold-prone pipes.	Autumn, before winter makes some repairs more difficult.	Medium to high to replace house piping. Low for fixing faucets, drains, toilets, insulating pipe. Low/medium for curing "hammer."
Change filter as needed. You may need to oil motor according to manufacturer's instructions. Balance uneven delivery by adjusting registers. Adjust blower belt.	Before cold weather arrives. May be cheaper and faster to get service call in summer.	Very low for new filters, oil for motor. Only your time to balance system. Medium/low for service calls.
Drain boiler water if rusty. Balance system at zone valves. Bleed air radiator/convectors. Check out and repair leaks.	Spring. Boilers are most prone to rusting in summer, when they aren't used.	Only your time to flush boiler, balance system, or bleed lines. Low to replace single section of pipe.
Make sure air vents are working, cant lines not tilted toward boiler. Flush rusty boiler water. Repair leaks.	Same as for hot water.	Only your time to purge air, cant lines, and flush boiler. Low to replace single pipe section.
Change the filter as needed. Hose debris from the outdoor condenser coils. Balance uneven delivery of cool air by adjusting registers.	Spring. A service call may be cheaper, faster in winter.	Very low for changing filters. Only your time for cleaning coil, balancing system. Medium/low for service calls.
Change filter as needed. Hose debris from outdoor condenser coil. May have to switch damper positions for heating, cooling modes. Switch on emergency heat when outdoor coil ices over and call for service.	Spring *and* autumn, because system runs continuously all year. Get off-season service calls.	Very low for changing filters. Your time for cleaning coil, rebalancing system for new seasons. Medium/low for service calls.

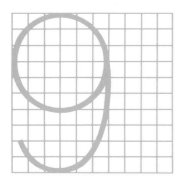

9
MINIMIZING MAINTENANCE

The house that requires absolutely no maintenance whatsoever has yet to be invented, but developments in easy-care materials have taken big strides in that direction. This chapter returns to areas of your home we've already explored—its yard, exterior, interior, and kitchen—and suggests improvements that can make maintenance easier.

MINIMIZING MAINTENANCE

THE YARD

Yard work can be a pleasure or a pain, an almost therapeutic endeavor or a seemingly endless chore. How it's regarded at your house depends on two things: what demands you make on the yard and what demands your yard makes on you. It's easy to assess the situation by asking one simple question: Is it worth it? If you believe you're investing more time, energy, and money in yard work than you're netting in enjoyment, it's time to make some changes.

Even if you've just moved into a brand-new house, you've probably inherited someone else's vision of what a yard should be. But just as you customize the inside of your home to suit your particular needs and tastes, you can do the same with outdoor spaces. To get the most from your little corner of the world, though, it's important to make it as easy as possible to care for. Otherwise, instead of enjoying what your yard has to offer, you'll end up resenting the sacrifices it asks you to make.

Start by assessing what's out there, looking first at the liabilities—shaded bare spots or well-worn paths in the lawn, awkward slopes, gangly and overgrown shrubs, tree branches that threaten electrical lines or fill gutters with leaves, and view-blocking bushes.

Next, decide what should go and what should stay. Remove trees with roots that jeopardize your home's foundation or basement. Cut back trees with branches that interfere with electrical lines or overhang the roof of your house or garage. If you ignore the latter, you'll face an annual chore of scooping wet leaves out of your gutters and downspouts. Prune tree branches that hang so low you have to duck to walk or mow under them. Tasks like these are usually one-time-only obligations. Take care of them now and you'll discover that your yard requires less maintenance than you anticipated.

Lightening lawn care

There's no getting around the fact that grass is a high-maintenance landscape amenity. It requires regular mowing, fertilizing, and weeding to look good. As with other home maintenance chores, the job is easier if you have the right tools. A fertilizer spreader can make feeding and weed-killing a relatively easy task. For large expanses of lawn, a self-propelled or tractor mower probably is worth the investment. Those equipped with grass catchers can eliminate the need for raking and bagging clippings and leaves.

Mowing still will be a major effort if you're confronted with an obstacle course. Can you get the mower under and around trees, shrubs, flower beds, and bushes? If not, regular mowing becomes that much more unpleasant and time-consuming. Obviously straight-line mowing is easiest, but you needn't eliminate all the flora to simplify the job. Thin out shrubs and bushes planted too close together, or transplant them to better locations to make faster, easier work of grass cutting. Fill in and reseed depressions. Move birdbaths and feeders from the yard to a flower bed. Use railroad ties, stones, bricks, or flexible borders around shrubs, bushes, trees, and flower beds to keep out the grass. Or, to cut down on the infestation of weeds and grass, spread a layer of wood chips or another suitable mulch around trees, shrubs, and flowers.

Finally, think about whether you really need all that grass. A deck made of redwood or pressure-treated wood can provide a low-maintenance surface and more usable outdoor space. Weather-resistant woods, which also make ideal fences, outdoor furniture, and planters, age gracefully and never need painting. Patios made of poured concrete or brick or stone pavers also can make your yard more usable, while reducing the area devoted to high-maintenance grass.

LAWN OPTIONS

Assess your requirements, then design a yard plan that will require as little maintenance as possible. Once you've decided how much open space you need, devote the rest of the yard to areas planted with ornamental trees, shrubs, hedges, and flower beds. Ask your nursery to recommend low-maintenance trees and shrubs, including some evergreens so that your yard will look as good during the winter as it does during the summer. Here are some other ways to cut your lawn down to size.
●Mulch under fences, as well as around flowers, trees, and shrubs, to simplify mowing and limit weed growth.
●Plant ground cover on slopes or in narrow side yards where mowing is difficult. Extend a deck out over a slope or terrace it so that it steps down in easy-to-mow intervals.
●With an in-ground sprinkler system, you won't have to haul out the hose every time you want to water the flowers or the grass. Where freezes are not a problem, lay rubber or plastic hose underground or conceal it beneath a layer of wood chips or gravel. In colder areas, use plastic pipe in a trench dug slightly deeper than the frost line.

MINIMIZING MAINTENANCE

OUTSIDE

Maintaining the exterior of an older home can sometimes seem a relentless, thankless job. Every fall the storm windows have to go up; in the spring they come down. Wood siding shrinks and splits with age, creating gaps that must be attended to. Old gutters begin to sag and eventually rust or rot away. Even after a brand-new paint job, the one thing you can be sure of is that you'll have to repaint in a few years. Sound familiar? If so, maybe it's time to think about ways to get off the maintenance treadmill. Here are some surefire ways to cut down on upkeep.

Modern houses wear better than older ones, thanks to low-maintenance skins that all but care for themselves. If you're faced with yet another paint job, maybe it's time to "pencil out" the economics of giving your home a new skin.

First, consider what you're about to pay the painter or paint store. (If you plan to do the job yourself, put a value on your labor.) Now estimate how many times you'll need to paint in the next, say, 20 years, and multiply this by the price of painting. Finally, compare this sum to the cost of re-siding your house with a minimal-maintenance material that won't need paint for at least 20 years.

Your pencil work will probably indicate that you'd be dollars ahead to re-side, but what about aesthetics? The good news here is that today's low-maintenance sidings have come a long way since the days of gunmetal-gray aluminum. Many are hardly distinguishable from wood, and several, in fact, *are* wood. The box at right summarizes your options.

Before you make a decision about the siding that's right for your house, examine what's underneath. Tight-fitting new siding reduces air infiltration, but it won't make up for lack of insulation and proper sheathing. If your home is leaking energy, you might be dollars ahead to strip walls to their sheathing or studs and upgrade insulation before the new siding goes up.

Siding isn't the only exterior component you can update. New roofing, windows, doors, gutters, and downspouts also offer ways to minimize maintenance. More about these, also, in the box at right.

EASY-CARE EXTERIORS

Investing in new surface materials can pay off with a lifetime of reduced maintenance. Here's a list that proves there's more than one way to skin a house.
- Aluminum siding offers a variety of lap, shingle, and vertical styles; a broad selection of colors; and several textures. Finishes are baked enamel or vinyl. Guarantees go up to 35 years for plastic-clad types.
- Steel siding costs more than aluminum and comes in a limited selection of lap and vertical styles. Color selection also is limited. Several makers offer lifetime guarantees.
- Vinyl siding is impervious to just about all perils, and because the color goes all the way through, it never needs painting. Vinyl costs more than any other type of siding and comes in only a limited selection of styles, textures, and colors.
- Cedar shingles and shakes can last 50 years and never need painting. They're relatively easy to apply, repair, and replace. Cost is moderate for shingles, expensive for shakes.
- Solid wood and plywood siding, available preprimed, presealed, or clad with vinyl, comes in many styles, textures, and finishes. Redwood and cedar naturally resist rot, so they never need painting. You can stain them or let them weather to a silvery gray.
- Hardboard siding comes in lap and vertical styles, with a variety of finishes and prefinished colors.

Some carry guarantees of up to 30 years. Others eventually need repainting.
- With roof shingles, you get just about as much durability as you're willing to pay for. Cheaper asphalt shingles last about 15 years and are prone to curling and cracking. Better-quality asphalt shingles carry guarantees of 25 years. Wood shingles and shakes are costly, and have a poor fire rating unless treated, but they last up to 50 years.
- Gutters and downspouts are available in wood, aluminum, galvanized steel, or vinyl. Wood and galvanized steel are the least expensive, but wood is prone to rot, galvanized steel to rusting—and both need periodic repainting. Aluminum and vinyl last longer—15 to 20 years for aluminum, a lifetime for vinyl.
- Thermal aluminum or vinyl-clad wood replacement windows have built-in screens and two or three panes of glass that reduce heat loss. Wood replacement windows are more costly than aluminum. If your home's windows are in decent condition, consider protecting them—and saving energy—with combination screen and storm windows. Combination windows are typically made of aluminum or steel. Steel costs more.
- Soffits, eaves, and window and door frames can be resurfaced with aluminum, by themselves or as part of an entire re-siding job. Cost is moderate.

MINIMIZING MAINTENANCE

INSIDE

There's no need to sacrifice style or good taste in order to keep the inside of your house looking good. With the right materials, you don't have to spend all your free time on housekeeping, either. Systematic, semiannual inspections, combined with a keep-it-simple philosophy applied to decorating and furnishings, will give you more time to enjoy the rooms in which you live.

Effectively and efficiently maintaining your home's interior spaces goes beyond routine housecleaning. Like outside maintenance, it requires more or less constant vigilance and, periodically, a thorough inspection. Still, you can accomplish both of these tasks in a minimum of time if you do them systematically and regularly.

Once or twice a year, make an attic-to-basement tour to detect and repair small problems before they turn into big ones. In the attic, check for roof leaks, fallen or loose insulation, window damage, and blocked vents. Also examine the chimney for signs of decay or smoke leakage.

In the basement, look for signs of dampness, particularly where the walls meet the floor, cracks in concrete block walls and floors, dripping plumbing joints, and cracked or decaying caulking around windows.

In the main rooms, examine all the windows, checking for deteriorating putty around glass panes, loose weather stripping, peeling paint on sills and sashes, malfunctioning locks, and air infiltration. Using high-gloss paint (instead of flat or satin-finish varieties) on windowsills and frames will make them more soil resistant and easier to clean. You may even want to consider applying plastic laminate to the sills. Also renew worn weather stripping and seals around exterior doors to keep out air and dust.

In the kitchen, make a habit of using the exhaust fan whenever you cook to keep airborne grease particles to a minimum. And change or clean the fan's filter frequently to keep it functioning efficiently. Use exhaust fans in bathrooms, too, to remove excess moisture, which can eventually damage wall surfaces and even your home's insulation. Cleaning or replacing the air filters in your forced-air furnace and air conditioner will help trap more dust and keep the inside of your house cleaner.

Reduce cleaning chores

If you really want to reduce the time it takes to clean your rooms, cut down on the things that get in the way of making a quick job of it. Keep furniture surfaces as clutter-free as possible. Store magazines in a rack or basket, books on shelves instead of on tables. Opt for just one or two decorative pillows on the sofa instead of piles of them.

When you shop for new furnishings, make upkeep an important consideration. Here are ways to further reduce cleaning chores.
- Replace fabric shades on lamps with plastic-coated paper shades that can be wiped off with a damp cloth.
- Choose short-nap carpeting, which is less prone to trapping dirt and dust.
- If you're in the market for upholstered furniture, consider pieces covered in leather or vinyl (some new vinyl upholstery is practically indistinguishable from leather and is much less expensive). Both are easy to maintain, and neither will contribute dust particles to the air in your home.

Obviously, the more streamlined your furniture, the easier it will be to clean. Intricate carvings, turned legs, and wicker or rattan frames are bound to trap more dirt and dust than smooth surfaces.

Finally, invest in the best possible vacuum cleaner you can afford, perhaps a self-propelled model if you have extensive areas of wall-to-wall carpeting. To make fast work of small jobs, buy a hand-held vacuum or an electric broom.

139

MINIMIZING MAINTENANCE

THE KITCHEN

Requiring daily, sometimes even hourly, attention, the kitchen is easily the most maintenance-intensive room in any home. If your kitchen is nearing the end of the line and you're thinking about installing a new one, you have an opportunity to cut the time devoted to kitchen-keeping by as much as 50 percent.

You probably already know what you don't like about your present kitchen, but as you plan a new one, make special note of the maintenance shortcomings that bother you most. Are you tired of wiping up around small appliances that are cluttering counters because there's simply not enough storage for them? Are there gaps around the range that trap food and attract insects? Does the floor seem to never come clean?

No kitchen will ever be totally maintenance-free, but good planning can make one almost a joy to take care of.

Cabinets

Plasticized finishes let you wipe cabinets clean with just a damp cloth or sponge. Available in traditional woods that are protected by a polyurethane coating or in even more durable plastic or metal laminates, low-maintenance cabinets never need painting.

As you evaluate a cabinet line's construction, also imagine what it would be like to clean and maintain them. Are there ornate carvings or moldings that might collect dirt and grease? Do hinges and catches look sturdy enough to withstand thousands of openings and closings? Do drawers move smoothly?

The way cabinets fit together in a kitchen also plays a part in how easy a new kitchen will be to maintain. Closely butted cabinets not only maximize storage, but they also present fewer side surfaces to clean. If your present kitchen doesn't have a soffit above the wall cabinets, you may have noticed that this area is a big dust-collector, useful for storing only seldom-used items. Including a soffit in your redesigned kitchen would eliminate one cleaning chore.

Counters

Counters bear the brunt of everyday spills and spatters, and no other kitchen surface has to be cleaned as often. Here are the maintenance pros and cons of countertop options.
- *Plastic*. Laminate, vinyl, and solid acrylic counters stand up well to grease and stains, and clean easily with soap and water. They can't tolerate high heat or sharp knives, however, and over the years they begin to dull and wear thin.
- *Wood*. Butcher block is the main contender, though you also can make a wood counter with oak or maple flooring. Wood can last a lifetime, but needs to be rubbed periodically with mineral oil and may need occasional sanding to remove deep stains or scars. Also, wood is not highly resistant to heat or water.
- *Hard-surface materials*. Tile, ceramic glass, stainless steel, and natural and synthetic marble countertops last indefinitely, and most are very easy to maintain. With tile, you need to periodically clean and seal the grouting. Stubborn spots on ceramic glass can be cleaned with a cleaner sold for smooth-top ranges. Stainless steel is prone to water spotting and scratches easily. Natural marble is porous and can absorb stains; synthetic marble is nonporous and much easier to maintain.

Floors

Floors have to stand up to many of the same punishments inflicted on counters, plus the dirt and wear and tear of foot traffic. Your options fall into four categories.
- *Resilient flooring* includes a variety of vinyl formulations—solid vinyl sheet goods and tiles, cushioned sheet vinyl, poured vinyl, and vinyl asbestos tiles. The easiest to maintain have no-wax surfaces; you simply damp-mop with mild detergent. High-grade cushioned sheet vinyl is the most durable; others are vulnerable to dents and require more frequent care.
- *Hard-surface flooring*—ceramic tile, quarry tile, slate, brick, marble, and terrazzo—lasts practically forever and needs only occasional damp-mopping. Some quarry tiles are porous and require a sealer. You need to wax slate, brick, and marble periodically. Grout joints may need occasional scouring and treatment with a mildew retardant.
- *Wood flooring* holds up well but needs daily vacuuming or dry-mopping. Attend to spills right away, removing stains with a cloth moistened in cleaner or wax. All but polyurethane-coated floors should be waxed periodically.
- *Carpeting* with nylon or polypropylene fibers wears well but should be vacuumed daily. Spills require immediate attention to prevent permanent stains. Nylon absorbs water slightly; polypropylene repels water. Don't use carpet tiles in kitchens because joints between the squares absorb water and stains.

Appliances

When you shop for appliances, go for the most streamlined models you can find and/or afford. Poorly positioned controls trap grease and dirt and require almost daily cleaning. Choose models with controls located in closable compartments or those designed to minimize maintenance. Steer away from appliances with an abundance of chrome strips and dust-catching ledges. (For more about choosing appliances, see pages 146 and 147 and 150–153.)

A GUIDE
TO EASY MAINTENANCE

For most of us, easy maintenance seems a contradiction in terms. Maintaining a home, after all, takes time, effort, and money, none of which is easy to come by nor easy to part with. If routine maintenance were truly easy, we'd probably call it recreation instead of work. But there are ways to make upkeep less laborious, less time-consuming, and less expensive. These same techniques also should give you more time, energy, and money to devote to enjoying your home. In the final analysis, maintenance is the price you pay for shelter, comfort, equity, housing, and a reasonable return on your investment.

Basically, easy maintenance consists of just three ingredients: the right attitude, the right equipment, and the right materials.

The right attitude

In other words, do it now. Procrastination is costly in every respect. Resolve to deal with those things that need immediate attention promptly and to devote a certain amount of time, effort, and money to regularly scheduled maintenance chores throughout the year. Evenly distributed over 12 months, routine fix-up tasks won't seem nearly so cumbersome. Let them pile up and you're bound to resent having to devote all your spare time to playing catch-up.

Once or twice a year, conduct a top-to-bottom survey of your house. Make a list of items that will need attention. Rank them according to importance. A sidewalk crack can wait awhile, but a broken window or a sagging gutter needs fixing now. Then you can devote a couple of summer weekends to remedying all the problems you've discovered or distribute the chores evenly over a few months. This technique also can help you budget for big-ticket items like a new roof or backyard deck.

The right equipment

Buy the best you can afford. That goes for the furnace, the water heater, the air conditioner, the lawn mower, the vacuum cleaner, the garden tools, and all the other mechanical items that can help make maintenance easier. Quality lasts, and in the long run it's usually worth the expense to spend more on a laborsaving tool that will help make quick work of home maintenance chores. A good self-propelled lawn mower that automatically bags grass clippings, for example, may cost more than a stripped-down version, but think of the time and effort it will save you over the years.

Things like self-cleaning ovens and frost-free refrigerators eliminate some maintenance tasks altogether. A new category of small appliances—can openers, toaster ovens, microwave ovens, coffee makers, even TVs—that mount to the undersides of kitchen cabinets can make daily kitchen counter maintenance much easier.

Of course, you could easily go bankrupt buying every laborsaving machine on the market. So, plan to invest in the right equipment, regularly supplementing your tools whenever the budget allows. Over a few short years, you'll have assembled an equipment collection that will make your life increasingly easier.

The right materials

The simple truth is, some materials just require less looking after and fewer repairs than others. Again, expense is a consideration, but so, too, are taste and common sense. It's not likely that anyone will replace the living room carpet with industrial flooring just because the latter is easier to clean.

Gradually you can replace some high-maintenance materials—clapboard siding, say—with low-maintenance materials such as aluminum or vinyl siding. When the time comes to replace worn materials, keep ease of maintenance in mind: no-wax vinyl flooring, washable and strippable wallpaper, and vinyl or aluminum gutters. Over a relatively short span of years your maintenance chores will decrease.

Any premium you pay for easy-maintenance materials amortizes itself as the years go by. Instead of merely collecting dividends on your investments,

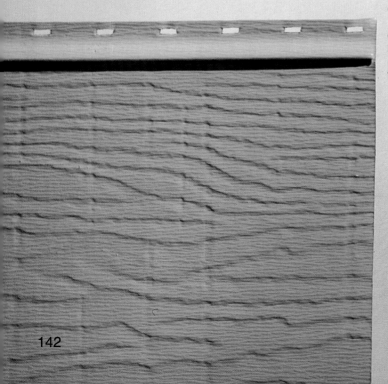

consider reinvesting them in *more* easy-maintenance materials. For example, the price of paint jobs you'll save over the years with low-maintenance siding could be considered when a new roof is needed. Then some of the money you've saved on paint jobs could be applied to roofing materials that will last a decade or longer than inexpensive roofing.

Naturally, you'll want to set some priorities. Think about which maintenance tasks you like least, then set out to eliminate them or to significantly reduce the effort they require. If, for example, you find yourself faced with the chore of repainting soffits and eaves every year or so, track down the cause of blistering and peeling paint (too little ventilation in the attic?) and then fix the problem. Or, consider installing aluminum soffits, gutters, or siding so you'll never have to paint.

Organize storage

Adequate storage lets you get things out of your way so that periodic cleaning goes faster. In the garage, build in storage shelves for paint cans, insecticides, and motor oil. Install hooks and hangers for everything from bicycles to garden tools. Put up pegboard and hang all your tools on it. Put down plywood over the ceiling joists so you can store lawn furniture in the garage's attic.

The same strategies also will work wonders in the basement. Inexpensive workshop vacuums may be worth the investment for both the garage and the basement, as well as two good push brooms and dust pans and two ample garbage cans. Equip both spaces with cleanup materials and you won't have to tote them back and forth (or try to remember where you left them).

Use the same techniques for high-maintenance rooms in the house, especially in the bathrooms, kitchen, utility room, or mudroom. Supply each of those rooms with their own cleansers, hand-held vacs, bench brooms and dustpans, sponges, and paper towels.

Then you can deal with disasters when they happen or simply do everyday cleaning when you notice it's needed. And you won't have to carry all your cleaning supplies with you.

Simply setting down some rules for family members also can cut down on the work involved in keeping your house in good order. Make the guest bath off limits to children; make the front entry off limits during wet weather; train dogs and cats to stay out of the living room; post a "take off your shoes" sign on the back door.

Finally, be ruthless when it comes to disposing of things you no longer need, use, or want. Take stock of the broken lawn chairs, the outgrown toys, the abandoned sled, the ancient golf clubs, and all the other miscellaneous castoffs that trip up the best-laid plans for easy maintenance.

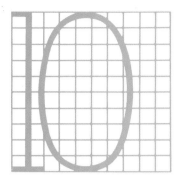

WHEN THINGS JUST WEAR OUT

In one sense, "maintenance" is a misleading term: Even the most scrupulously conscientious homeowner won't be able to "maintain" things forever. When an appliance's time has come, it's time to replace it. This chapter outlines some basic advice on how to do just that: how to cope with the inevitability of failure, how to shop for major components and appliances, how to buy (energy-) efficiently, what to know about warranties, and how to get new components and appliances up and running.

COPING WITH MURPHY'S LAW

If things can go wrong, they will. After all, it's Murphy's Law. Mr. and Mrs. Homeowner, meet Mr. Murphy.

If there's an implicit understanding among American homeowners, it's that things have no right to go awry, and that they should always do what they were intended to do, especially large, *expensive* mechanical things. When they don't do what they were meant to do, the reaction often is a lot of screaming, shouting, and hurt feelings. It may vent frustrations, but the thing is no closer to being fixed than it was before.

When things break down, fall apart, or just wear out, how you react is the single most important step on the way to making them right again—by far. And react is the correct word. Keeping a cool head won't make your balky washing machine work again, but it will help you zero in on what the problem is and how you can solve it. And you're more likely to keep a cool head if you have a plan already in hand to deal with household crises.

Relying on yourself

When a major appliance or component falls victim to Murphy's Law, your immediate inclination may be to call someone to repair it. (And your next thought is probably something like, "Well, there goes the budget. No fun weekends for a while.")

Usually, it's a better idea to resist the urge and try other solutions first. If you're methodical at this point, you may find the answer more quickly—and less expensively—than you would with a service call.

To begin with, make a practice of saving everything about components and their maintenance histories: owners' manuals, installation instructions, warranties, descriptions of past repairs, and the like. Most important, store all the documents so you can find what you need without turning the house upside down.

At the same time, don't assume that things aren't responding for complex reasons you'll never discover. Often, the solution is blessedly simple. Loose plugs, tripped switches or blown fuses, improperly set controls, and similar nuisances aren't really problems at all. A few seconds of your attention, and you're back in business.

If the obvious isn't the answer, making repairs yourself isn't out of the question, provided you have the skills. At times like these, experienced do-it-yourselfers understand the value of taking a disciplined, organized approach, rather than whirling into the job, creating a welter of parts, and getting lost in a profusion of screws, washers, and other hardware. Lay out a step-by-step approach to the work—on paper, if necessary—and be sure you understand how to put everything back together again.

Finally, know what you're about to get into, or at least have a pretty good idea. Now isn't the time to be a bold explorer, unless you're prepared for a learning experience or are solely interested in discovery for discovery's sake. If you've been all thumbs from birth, or if you're a mechanical nitwit with no interest in doing it yourself, then good help—professional help—is what you'll need.

Service, please

Uninterested or unskilled individuals aren't the only people who have to rely on professional help. Even the handiest and heartiest do-it-yourselfers require expert service on occasion. When the time comes, knowing whom to call can make all the difference.

Whom *do* you call? Service representatives have no better allies than satisfied customers. Check first with friends, neighbors, relatives, co-workers, any trustworthy source who's had similar problems and come away smiling.

If you're not able to find useful recommendations, contact the company that sold you the product (another reason to keep careful records), and find

out if it has a service department. Some retailers—the larger ones—do; most don't, however. If the retailer doesn't, ask for the names of the repair shops that install the store's products and do work under warranty for it.

Manufacturers themselves are another possibility. Factory-style outlets or small firms advertising repair of one or more manufacturers' brand-name products are often likely candidates. Further, many major manufacturers operate toll-free hotlines to provide immediate help. (You'll find a listing of some on pages 156 and 157.) Ordinarily, the operator will relay the names and numbers of service representatives in your area and perhaps other advice, as well. If it's truly an emergency, you'll probably have to trust the reference and make a call to one of the shops; as a rule, you won't go wrong. In most cases, however—whether you have a surefire recommendation or not—it's wise to check with the Better Business Bureau before arranging for repairs.

When you've found help, handle the matter as you might if you were having a major job done on your automobile by a

mechanic you've heard good things about but who, nevertheless, has never worked on your car before.

Always start with an estimate, and for big jobs, a written estimate. Often, finding the problem is a task in itself. Some professionals charge a fee if they have to spend a certain amount of time making a diagnosis, and some may even want to take your ailing machine back to the shop. In any event, don't agree to extensive repairs before you see an estimate in writing. Also, make sure there's an understanding that the repair person will contact you if the final bill will be higher than the estimate.

When the work is finished, ask for an itemized invoice, detailing the cost of labor and, more important perhaps, listing each new part that was installed. Some savvy, very careful homeowners even request the old parts as a double check.

During all of the give and take, it's wise to be cordial but direct. Most reputable repair shops will understand your businesslike approach; the best, in fact, may well expect it. It's definitely not smart, however, to hover around dispensing advice while a professional is working. Competent professionals will pump you for as many details as they can about the machine's maintenance history and its current state of disrepair. When you've filled

them in on the background, take a step *into* the background, appearing only to answer additional questions.

Finding skilled service representatives—people who also do their jobs on time and at a fair price—is a wonderful discovery. Once you know who they are, never let them go, because Murphy's Law is always active, and you'll undoubtedly need their help again—and again.

REPLACING MAJOR APPLIANCES

No matter how well you cope with Murphy's Law and all its corollaries, you'll have to replace major components eventually. It's as simple, and as complicated, as that.

Once you're in the market, you'll find a sizable, sometimes overwhelming, array of choices, along with enough low- and high-tech options to fill several catalogs. In the long run, that variety is good, because it means you're likely to find just what you and your family need, and at an affordable price.

In the short run, though, it means you must be or become an informed consumer to get the best deal possible. These pages present basic buymanship information for important household components. Use it as a starting point in your search, then turn to other parts of this chapter for advice on energy considerations (pages 150 and 151), guarantees and warranties (pages 152 and 153), getting the work done (pages 154 and 155), and financing the purchase (page 155).

Start your quest at a local library, where you'll find books and consumer publications that rate or describe brand-name appliances. You'll pick up a wealth of data on features, prices, and performance. Jot down facts, zero in on three or four candidates that look good on paper, and then call area retailers to see if they have what you're after. You might even be able to get a price over the phone.

Here, starting in the kitchen, is a survey of the choices you'll find on today's market.

Refrigerators

Refrigerators are expensive on the showroom floor, and they're expensive to operate. The key to getting the right one for your family is to avoid getting stuck with too much storage capacity. A serviceable rule is 12 cubic feet of refrigerator and freezer space for a two-person household, plus two extra cubic feet for each additional family member.

Obviously, a refrigerator has to fit into its surroundings, so measure the area where you plan to put it. Remember that some models run efficiently only if there's space for air to circulate at the top, back, or sides.

Refrigerators come in three basic styles. Single-door units carry the lowest price tags and are the most economical to operate, but they have to be defrosted by hand. Most two-door refrigerators, with the freezer either above or below, defrost automatically and, unlike their one-door counterparts, are able to store frozen food almost indefinitely. So can side-by-side models, which feature a door on one side and one or two doors on the other. They make food easily accessible but have narrower shelves.

To standard styles you can add a bevy of options, which, in turn, add to the purchase price. The most sought-after include: ice water dispensers; separate temperature controls for individual compartments; decorative door panels, some of them interchangeable; and automatic ice cube makers.

(An ice maker requires a minor plumbing hookup that can increase the overall cost of the refrigerator.)

Freezers

Consider another rule of thumb for freestanding freezers: 3 or 4 cubic feet of space per person. Chest freezers open from the top; they're less costly and operate more efficiently, but nearly all need manual defrosting. Upright units, though more expensive to buy and run, make it simpler to find stored food and take up less room. Many models also defrost automatically. Here, too, you can select from among a range of optional features. One of the most popular is a "power on" light, which tells you at a glance if the freezer is doing its job.

Ranges, ovens, and cooktops

Today, manufacturers offer a broad range of options and configurations to make cooking more enjoyable and less time-consuming. For these appliances, too, take the measure of your kitchen, carefully noting relevant dimensions. In addition, settle on an energy source (usually gas or electricity). For the most part, it's more economical to stay with what you have, unless switching allows you to reap sizable savings over time.

Freestanding ranges are old standbys. Normally 30 inches wide and 3 feet high, they have ample storage space or large broilers below. So-called over/under double-oven ranges feature a second oven built atop a standard 30-inch-wide unit.

Slide-in ranges are just freestanding models minus the side panels. They're made to fit comfortably between cabinets. Generally, backsplashes and a single side panel—if only one side is covered—are options.

Unlike slide-in units, drop-in or built-in ranges (with an oven below) are permanently positioned inside cabinets. They're ideal for island counters and are easy to operate because the broiler's at waist height. For similar reasons, single or double built-in ovens also are popular, as are cooktops, which are basically gas or electric ranges built into a countertop.

As millions already have discovered, quick-working microwave ovens (portable, built-in, or linked to a conventional unit) can cook food from 60 to 75 percent faster than ordinary models, with commensurate savings in energy costs. Convection ovens, energy-efficient gas ranges, glass ceramic cooktops, and magnetic induction cooktops all save energy in one way or another, so they're less costly than standard models over the long haul. Initially, however, all are comparatively expensive models or features.

As you shop for a range or oven, one important choice you have to make is whether you want the oven to be self-cleaning or continuous cleaning, or have an old-fashioned porcelain-coated metal interior you clean yourself. Each has its advantages and disadvantages.

• *Self-cleaning ovens* have an 800-plus-degree temperature cycle that incinerates even stubborn spills into powdery ash residues that you simply wipe out with a damp rag or sponge. Self-cleaning ovens cost considerably more than other types and some, especially gas versions, are smaller inside.

• *Continuous-cleaning ovens* have porous interior coatings that gradually burn off minor spills at normal oven temperatures. You still have to wipe up heavy spills shortly after they occur and conventional oven cleaners can spoil the special surface.

• *Porcelainized metal ovens* require more cleaning effort than either of the other types, but add nothing to the price of the range. Also, with oven cleaner, you can make them sparkle again and again without damaging their interiors.

Dishwashers
Either built-in or portable, they're usually 24 inches wide, 24 inches deep, and 35 inches high, though smaller and larger versions aren't hard to find. Built-ins fit into space beneath a countertop and are tied into the house plumbing. Portable, roll-away models attach to a faucet and then drain through the sink.

Whichever you select—portable or built-in—be sure to pick a model large enough to accommodate at least a day's worth of dishes. In addition to adequate size, a good dishwasher should be made of durable, rustproof material; should be easy to load; and should have an effective strainer and filter to keep food particles from gumming up the works.

Dishwashers, like other appliances, come with lots of options. Among the most use-ful: soft-food disposers, which eliminate the need to rinse most dishes before washing; timed dispensers to release detergent and additives at set intervals; and preheating cycles that allow you to dial down the temperature of your water heater and still get perfectly clean dishes and utensils.

The total cost of a dishwasher mainly depends on how many types of washing cycles the machine has—from rinse-and-hold to a delay-wash cycle that automatically turns the unit on at a programmed time—after you've gone to bed, for example.

Garbage disposers
Again, you have two major types to choose from. So-called batch-feed units dispose of waste in batches at a time—anywhere from 1½ to 2 quarts—and operate via a built-in switch that's triggered when the drain lid is set in place. By contrast, continuous-feed disposers, ordinarily activated by a wall switch, can gobble up garbage while they work. Good models of either kind include a dependable motor with a minimum of ½ horsepower, an automatic reversing function, and parts that resist corrosion.

Washers and dryers
Unlike the bad old days, washers and dryers now come outfitted to handle clothes of every kind, and save energy in the process.

Well-equipped washers boast some or all of these features: variable wash cycles, water-level controls, separate temperature controls for wash and rinse cycles, automatic soak cycles, and extra-fast spin cycles.

As a rule, both gas- and electric-powered dryers are controlled by a timer, which cycles clothes through a predetermined number of minutes. More expensive and energy-efficient models are regulated by an electronic sensor, which automatically stops the unit when the clothes are dry. Any model, however, should have a powerful door catch, safety controls that shut off the appliance when the door is open, and easily accessible filters, which need regular cleaning.

Water heaters
Size is crucial. Purchase a unit that's too small, and you're plagued by a lack of hot water; buy one that's too large, and you're burdened with unnecessarily high energy bills. Typical families can make do with a 40-gallon heater.

A water heater's recovery rate—or the amount of water it can warm in a half hour or hour—is also important if your family uses a lot of hot water at certain times of the day. A heater that "recovers" rapidly assures that no one is stuck with a chilly shower.

When you're shopping for a water heater, determine, also, how well its tank is insulated. The less heat a tank loses, the less energy it consumes. Well-insulated tanks generally last longer, too, because they expand and contract less during heating cycles.

Finally, for maximum energy savings, consider coupling a modern, high-efficiency, well-insulated water heater with a solar unit. More about this on page 151.

More about this on page 151.

SELECTING APPLIANCES FOR A DISABLED PERSON

Choosing kitchen appliances for a wheelchair-bound person, especially someone who plans to use the appliances extensively, takes a little common sense and an appreciation of how that individual deals with things around him.

First and foremost, keep safety features in mind when you're shopping. Conventional free-standing ranges, for example, are not ideal choices. Instead, consider cooktops, with controls at the front and burners or heating elements staggered so the wheelchair-user won't have to reach across an element in front to place a pot on a unit in back.

Similarly, wall-mounted ovens are often ideal choices for disabled people, as are microwave units that open from the side rather than the top. These appliances can be placed at heights easily reached by a wheelchair-user.

Well-adapted refrigerators are also a necessity. Think about getting one with slide-out drawers and a slide-out freezer at the bottom. In addition, inspect the doors carefully before you buy. Some are so wide that they actually become barriers to disabled individuals.

WHEN THINGS JUST WEAR OUT

REPLACING HEATING AND COOLING EQUIPMENT

Most heating and cooling equipment is designed to provide decades of trustworthy service. Properly maintained, it will carry on with nary a thought from you.

Nevertheless, final breakdowns are inevitable, and predicting them is essential. An aged furnace that comes to a wheezing end in the dead of winter signals a true household emergency. Buying new components under such pressure is usually a lightning-fast, haphazard decision, which, given the cost of energy and the array of economical alternatives available, many homeowners quickly learn—and live—to regret.

From time to time, it's a good idea to call in a skilled heating or cooling contractor; when the contractor starts suggesting expensive repairs rather than routine maintenance, it's a good cue for you to start shopping around.

Heating components

Being in the market for a new furnace or boiler has one big advantage—theoretically, at least. It gives you a chance to compare different kinds of energy—typically oil, natural gas, and electricity—and then make a change if the cost of one is lower than the fuel you've been paying for.

Generally, however, common perceptions about relative costs hold true—electricity is more expensive than oil, and oil is more costly than gas. Many experts now recommend switching only if you can identify clearly significant savings

(as many homeowners did by moving from oil to natural gas during the dark days of the energy crisis). Nevertheless, your choice is often determined as much by the local or regional availability of energy as it is by the cost of using that fuel.

Sizing equipment properly is perhaps a clearer, more identifiable decision, one that can mean equally clear-cut savings. It's possible that all you need is a furnace or boiler capable of matching the old unit's output (in BTUs, a measure of heat produced, per hour).

Chances are, however, that the existing heater is either pumping out too much warmth or too little. If you've added on in recent years, it's probably the latter. On the other hand, many older homes are heated by furnaces or boilers that were intentionally oversized to begin with, expensive remnants of an era when energy was cheap.

During the coldest winter days, heating plants with the correct capacity are running almost constantly; ones that are too large seem to cycle on and off a lot. In any event, an assessment from an up-to-date heating contractor—they're trained nowadays not to be so generous with their specifications—is ordinarily a wise investment.

In addition, reliable pros will gladly fill you in on the technical details, advantages, and

disadvantages of different units. The whole field of heating technology has changed—and is changing—so rapidly that well-informed advice at the time you're in the market is almost an essential key to selecting components that'll work best for you. The following is sound general advice about major kinds of heating plants, components, and accessories.

• *Styles*. Oil, gas, and electric heaters come in four basic styles, or shapes. (Gas and oil units tend to be about the same size. Electric heaters of the same style are usually more compact.) The so-called upflow highboy is by far the most common, in part because it's not very wide or deep, which means it can be tucked away in closets, utility rooms, or out-of-the-way corners of the basement.

In contrast, the lowboy is built close to the ground and is a good choice in houses where headroom is hard to come by. In older homes, which sometimes have little space below, remodelers often install lowboys when they're replacing ancient equipment.

Counterflow models are much like highboys, with a few design differences that make them ideal candidates for crawl spaces or homes where duct systems are buried in concrete.

Finally, horizontal units, which, as the name suggests, take up little vertical space, are highly versatile. They can be positioned in crawl spaces, installed in attics, or even hung from the rafters.

• *Heat pumps*. Once all the rage among homeowners, these electric-powered units are, in effect, air-conditioning in reverse. Most, in fact, can be used as central cooling units during the summer. During the winter, the pump, which works with a standard compressor, removes warmth from outside air (even the coldest air has plenty of heat to give up) and brings it indoors. Although the equipment's efficiency falls as the temperature does, backup electric heaters begin to take up the slack at around 15 degrees Fahrenheit.

In general, pumps are more economical than other kinds of electric heating; nevertheless, sizing them is sometimes a problem, and, compared to other equipment, maintaining them is usually more time-consuming.

• *Zoned heating*. Zoning, which applies to cooling as well, allows different rooms or areas of the house to be heated at different temperatures, or not heated at all, an obviously money-saving virtue and something frequently done when major equipment is being replaced.

Some heating systems are much more zonable than others. For example, hot-water systems are generally the easiest to zone and usually yield the most satisfactory results. In contrast, electric-resistance systems can be zoned, but ordinarily by individual rooms only. Zoning forced-air arrangements is not only more expensive, it occasionally adversely affects the entire system's balance, making whole rooms or parts of the house less, not more, comfortable.

• *Energy-efficient units.* In times past, most heating plants did the job, but wastefully so, gobbling up energy at the beginning and end of individual cycles, especially the end. (Energy lost when a burner shuts off and cools down is the biggest contributor to inefficiency.)

Today, manufacturers are constantly devising furnaces and boilers that rely on a variety of technological developments designed to use fuel as stingily as possible or retain energy that otherwise might go untapped.

Ordinarily, these units carry higher price tags than their older, energy-guzzling counterparts, but, depending on how finely tuned they really are, the payback period can be pleasantly swift, particularly for gas and oil burners. Expert advice from a trustworthy heating pro about features and how they work (nowadays, many are controlled by microprocessors) can go a long way and help save a lot of money.

• *Other options.* Forced-air systems warm and pump out vast amounts of dry heat, which, lacking much moisture, can prove both uncomfortable and unhealthy. Furnaces equipped with power humidifiers solve the problem. Some have motorized units that deliv-

er a very fine spray directly into the airflow; others contain a rotating waterwheel that throws off moisture as it circles through already heated air. In either case, the best models are regulated by a humidistat that automatically measures moisture levels and shuts the humidifier off when a preset point is reached.

Eiectronic whole-house air cleaners are often worthwhile extras, as well. They're capable of removing most of the airborne pollutants that elude a heater's filter.

Finally, when replacing major equipment, install an energy-saving setback thermostat as well. It will automatically lower a thermostat's setting for one or more periods each day.

Cooling off

Like heating units, air-conditioning equipment must be sized accurately to operate efficiently and economically. And, like heating plants installed when energy was inexpensive, older models or systems may be wastefully oversized (or, in some cases, uncomfortably undersized). A thorough evaluation by a skilled cooling contractor (or several if you're taking bids) can tell you where the hot spots are in your home and how quickly the whole structure heats up—knowledge that can serve as a useful guide to selecting new equipment.

Because pros understand that it's tough to exactly match cooling power and a room's or home's heat gain, most recommend that the system or unit be slightly undersized, a fact that affects comfort levels only moderately.

For central air-conditioning, a contractor also can evaluate other integral parts of the system (plenum, blower, branch ducts) to determine if they're adequately sized. Sometimes, they're too small or underpowered to cool as efficiently as they might.

The best basic type of central air-conditioning (for houses, anyway) is the so-called split system, which allows the always-noisy compressor and the condenser coils to be installed on a concrete slab outside the house, with the evaporating coils placed inside. Runs of small copper tubing connect the two components.

Some systems have multiple-speed condensing units, which are economical options because they allow you to fine-tune the volume of cooled air being delivered and reduce demand when you choose. Though the majority of central air-conditioning systems are powered by electricity, gas-fueled units also are available. Ordinarily, they're more costly to install, but operating expenses are usually lower and maintenance simpler than with electric models.

Prices for central systems often vary quite a bit, even for components with similar capacities. Quality comes into play here. Some units putting

out the same volume of cooled air will simply continue to do the job much longer than others delivering the same output. Again, expert advice will help identify those with longer life spans.

Room air conditioners, which operate on electricity only, are—output for output—less efficient than central systems, and most pros don't suggest installing a series of them to do what central air does better: cool an entire house. Even so, for handling specific areas, they're the way to go, and, run conservatively, a set of room units totaling the same capacity can even be less expensive to operate than central air-conditioning. What's more, installation costs are much lower.

Though many room models are designed for conventional double-hung windows, other types are readily available: models for casement windows, models for consoles that rest in front of windows, and models that fit into wall openings (often these are the best, because they don't block the view and because they typically run less noisily).

Finally, some room units are more efficient than others. When you're in the market, compare efficiency ratings carefully. You'll find that the most efficient models are often the most sophisticated, as well, with controls featuring built-in timers or switches that allow you to operate the fan when the compressor is off.

SHOPPING FOR ENERGY SAVINGS

Although major appliances and components don't consume as much energy as, say, uninsulated attics, they nevertheless can account for up to 20 percent of your total fuel bill, sometimes more. For well over 10 years, manufacturers have been catering to the energy-saving conscience of the American homeowner, which in practical terms translates into a wealth of products designed to work as efficiently as possible.

Bargain models or "economy" buys are easy-on-the-pocketbook dazzlers when you see them on the showroom floor, but, with certain exceptions (refrigerators are one), they're often energy guzzlers compared to more expensive alternatives in the same product line. No matter how solidly they're constructed or how dependably they do their jobs, operating them over a period of years may, in fact, prove to be far more costly than buying an energy-saver at the start.

Refrigerators, freezers

Refrigerators eat more energy than any other kitchen appliance and, in most households, rank second only to water heaters in a tally of annual operating costs.

That knowledge alone should prompt you to look for a refrigerator sized to fit your family's needs (see pages 146 and 147). Misfit models burn up energy day and night (refrigerators never sleep), and underused compartments have to work harder to cool their contents.

In one sense, single-door units are proportionately more costly to run than two-door and side-by-side models because energy escapes from both freezer and cooler each time you open the door. Even so, because they're manually defrosted, single-door refrigerators require much less electricity to operate—as much as 50 percent less—than units with automatic defrosters, savings you'll gain for any model that has to be defrosted by hand. In fact, the more "convenient" your refrigerator becomes, the more expensive it ultimately becomes, as well. Ice makers, cold-beverage dispensers, and similar features take power to keep up and running, and they, too, are running constantly.

Two energy-efficient features are worth considering. One is commonly called a power-saver switch; it turns off the heating element buried in metal or plastic around the refrigerator's door opening. In hot, humid weather this element minimizes condensation problems. In cool, dry periods you don't need it. Used wisely, variable-temperature controls also can be energy-savers because they allow you to vary the temperature compartment by compartment, depending on the kind of food you're storing.

Where you position a new refrigerator also has something to do with how efficiently it operates. The old location may not, in fact, be the best, especially if it's on an uninsulated exterior wall that's exposed to the sun. Similarly, to work properly, some models need breathing space around the sides, back, and top.

Whenever you open a free-standing freezer, you get a shot of cold air and lose a little money in the process. On the average, chest freezers are more energy-efficient than upright units. Like refrigerators, neither is at its best if you don't keep it well stocked with frozen goods.

Cooking appliances

Unlike refrigerators and freezers, which have to be on duty at all times, modern ovens and ranges offer sizable energy-saving potential. Equipped with the right controls, they can be fine-tuned to do their jobs effectively yet efficiently, operating at levels that older or less high-tech models simply can't equal.

For example, conventional gas stoves with pilot lights are woefully big energy robbers; the flame's on, whether you're cooking or not, and typically accounts for a third to a half of the gas used to operate the unit. Models with electric or electronic ignition systems use fuel only when you're using the appliance.

Likewise, ranges and ovens with programmed controls automatically turn down gas or electricity at precisely the right moment, holding food at a comfortable serving temperature, freeing you from bondage in the kitchen, and saving you money in the process.

Aside from energy-efficient options, whole units that make use of quicker but just as effective cooking methods also

are available, at prices that continue to come down. Though initially more expensive, many are ultimately bargain buys because of the money saved on unused gas or electricity.

- *Convection ovens.* These units are equipped with a blower that circulates heated air around food, which can be readied at lower temperatures and in less time (no preheating is necessary).
- *Glass ceramic cooktops.* Not only energy-savers but also wonderfully easy to clean, these units feature surfaces that cool slowly and finish cooking the food after you've shut off the power.
- *Magnetic induction cooktops.* They prepare food quickly and cook it evenly, but they never get hot, something that makes cleaning the surface a snap. One disadvantage: You can use only iron or steel cookware.
- *Microwave ovens.* These units rely on high-frequency radio waves to get the job done, which they do much more speedily than conventional ovens and at a fraction of the cost. Smaller units can work off ordinary household power (110 to 120 volts); larger ones, however, require their own 220-volt circuits, as do other major cooking appliances that use electricity. Combination microwave and conventional ovens or microwave and convection ovens are highly versatile creations. Used together (or separately), the microwave hastens cooking and the conventional or convection unit browns food, a finishing touch many microwave ovens are unable to perform.

Dishwashers

In general, using a dishwasher consumes energy at an only slightly greater rate than doing the same job by hand—and if you're not careful to turn off the hot water when you're not rinsing, manual washing can gobble *more* energy than a machine does.

Look for a dishwasher with a setting that automatically shuts off the unit after the rinse cycle, leaving the dishes to air-dry and saving up to a third on operating costs as a result. And once the dishwasher is installed, use it conservatively. Don't activate the controls until there's a full load inside, and avoid using the rinse-hold cycle as much as possible. It's a consummate hot-water waster.

Washers and dryers

Manufacturers have taken mighty strides in making these two major appliances as energy-efficient as possible. In addition to the features noted on pages 146 and 147, consider the following during your search for replacements:
- *Bleach dispensers.* They enhance a washer's cleaning abilities when it's operating with cold water.
- *Suds-saving controls.* These allow you to automatically route wash water into a nearby storage tub, hold it there during the rinse-and-spin cycle, and then bring it back into the washer for the next wash cycle.

- *Electric ignition systems.* As they do in a kitchen oven or range, electric ignition systems fire up a gas dryer only when it needs the power.

Remember, too, that different washers use different amounts of water, and sometimes the difference is considerable. Less thirsty units will conserve hot water and keep money in your pocket.

Water heaters

These are the kingpins of household energy consumption, and it'll make sense to choose them carefully and use them efficiently.

Determining the right size is the single most important step toward picking the right heater (see pages 146 and 147). The second is selecting one that's properly insulated. Although conventional models with thick insulation on the shell are more expensive than other kinds, the energy they save can be substantial, enough to make up the difference in sales-floor price tags very quickly.

Above all, once a heater's in place and doing its job, don't let it work too hard if you don't need the effort. In a household with no dishwasher (or one that preheats the water), there are few good reasons to set a heater at 140 degrees Fahrenheit, rather than 120, which should be adequate.

At the same time, drain the unit regularly; doing so will increase its efficiency. Think, too, about insulating hot-water supply lines. In some cases, energy savings will make up the cost in six months or less.

Because gas or electric water heaters are *so* expensive to operate, solar-powered

heaters are proving to be practical choices, especially in the Sun Belt, but in many northern states, as well. To serve the growing demand, manufacturers have developed a variety of active and passive systems, which they're constantly refining. Depending in part on climate, some are able to satisfy all of a household's hot-water needs, and most can take care of at least 50 percent.

Compared to conventional choices, even the simplest solar heaters are costly, with outlays of $1,500 to $2,000 not uncommon. Complicated or extensive systems can easily total $8,000 or more. Many homeowners have discovered, however, that the payback in energy savings can be pleasantly swift: three to five years, sometimes sooner.

Let the labels lead you

Back in the mid- to late '70s, the federal government got into the energy business in a big way. One result was the Energy Policy and Conservation Act, which required manufacturers to place bright yellow-and-black labels or stickers, containing estimated annual operating costs, on most major appliances, including washers, dryers, freezers, ranges and ovens, refrigerators, and water heaters. The labels also showed energy-efficiency ratings, which allowed you to make comparisons among similar appliances. The higher the number, the greater the energy efficiency. The act has expired, but many manufacturers still use the yellow labels.

CONSERVING APPLIANCE ENERGY

Little things sometimes make the difference between manageable energy bills and unmanageably high expenses. Try the following tactics.
- *In the kitchen.* Cover cookware; you'll use less energy and do the job more quickly. Keep burners and reflectors clean. Turn off electric ranges and ovens at least five minutes before the scheduled cooking time; their heating elements will finish the job as they cool down. Don't open and close oven doors while you're waiting for food to cook. If you own them, rely on pressure cookers or microwave ovens. They cook food in a snap, using less power in the process.

Warm up the refrigerator to 40 degrees Fahrenheit in the main compartment and 5 degrees in the freezer. Manual-defrost models use less energy than their automatic cousins, but require regular defrosting.
- *In the laundry room.* Avoid large doses of detergent, and presoak or use the soak cycle to wash really dirty clothes.

Clean out the dryer's lint filter frequently, and make sure the outside exhaust stays unclogged. Dry heavy items in one load; lighter items, in a second one.

READING GUARANTEES AND WARRANTIES

"I guarantee it!" is an old—and notoriously unreliable—promise. Fortunately, though, it's one that most brand-name manufacturers of household appliances live up to every day of the year.

If you've done your homework properly and dealt with a reputable retailer recommended by family or friends, you'll probably walk away with an appliance or component that will work unfailingly from the minute you turn it on until it dies a natural death years later. You'll get what you wanted and what you paid for.

However, there may be a time when even the most diligently researched purchase yields a lemon—something that you wanted and paid for but that doesn't work. Then it'll make sense to know something about warranties (also called guarantees); they're your first, and best, recourse when things go wrong.

Promises, promises
Three types of warranties exist, and they definitely differ in scope: how you're covered, what's covered, and who's covered.

• *Full warranties.* These grant you a bundle of rights, and, in most cases, they're the protection you're looking for. To use the word "full" in its warranties, a manufacturer must agree—must legally promise—to do certain things should you run into problems in the first 90 days, 6 months, 1 year, or whatever period of time is specified in the coverage.

To begin with, the company promises to fix or replace a malfunctioning product at no charge and within a reasonable amount of time (this, too,

is described in the warranty). In addition, it promises not to set up unusually high hurdles when you're trying to have the product repaired or replaced (like recrating a heavy, unwieldy washer and dragging it to a designated service center miles away). At the same time, it promises to extend the same protections to anyone who owns the product during the covered period, although some full warranties don't contain this provision.

Finally, a full warranty promises to give you an important option, again, within a designated time. If the product really turns out to be a lemon and can't be repaired by even the finest technical minds, you get your money back, or you get a new product. In practice, most consumers take the latter.

Though strong remedies, full warranties aren't always a cure for problems that might arise after you buy a product, and on occasion, they're no help at all. Some, for example, cover only certain parts, leaving others unprotected. Reading the warranty in full, even a heavily promoted "full" warranty, is the only way to find out.

• *Limited warranties.* In general, limited guarantees are weaker promises, yet they can be trustworthy if you know what you're getting into.

As the name suggests, the protections are confined, or limited, to the terms described in the warranty. Some can be all-inclusive; others, nebulously misleading. Again, the only

TYPICAL APPLIANCE WARRANTY TERMS

APPLIANCE	WARRANTIES
REFRIGERATORS AND FREEZERS	One year for parts and labor; five years for compressor and other sealed refrigeration components.
RANGES	One year for parts and labor.
MICROWAVE OVENS	One year for parts and labor; five years for magnetron parts.
DISHWASHERS	One year for parts and labor; some manufacturers also warrantee that the tub won't crack or rust for up to 10 years.
TRASH COMPACTORS	One year for parts and labor.
AIR CONDITIONERS	One year for parts and labor; five years for the compressor and other sealed refrigeration.
WASHERS	One year for parts and labor.
DRYERS	One year for parts and labor.
WATER HEATERS	One year for parts and labor; up to 10 years against tank failure.

way to discover what's covered and what's not, and for how long, is to read the terms, front to back.

In most cases, however, you'll find that limited warranties don't promise or deliver as much protection as full guarantees. For example, if your brand-new washer breaks down and it's covered by a limited warranty, as a rule, only parts are covered, not labor. Similarly, limited warranties usually can't be transferred, and if you have to return the product to the manufacturer, it's often at your expense. Moreover, limited guarantees rarely provide for return of the full purchase price; prorated refunds are standard. Finally, some products may carry full warranties that extend only to a few heavy-duty, typically durable parts, with the others covered by carefully hedged limited guarantees.

• *Implied warranties.* Manufacturers don't *have* to provide *any* warranties. Today, however, many realize that it's purely good business to back up their products with legal promises. Just as obviously, however, components or appliances not covered by written guarantees aren't necessarily bad buys, nor are consumers who purchase them left entirely unprotected should defects materialize.

Unlike full and limited guarantees, implied warranties are unwritten promises, but promises nevertheless. To lawyers, they're called "warranties of merchantability" or "implied warranties of merchantability," meaning, in everyday language, that the manufacturer (and sometimes, the retailer,

as well) agrees the product is able to do what it's supposed to do—a water heater is able to heat water, for example, or a dishwasher is able to clean dishes. If it breaks down shortly after you bring it home and can't perform what it's made to do, then—legally—the seller is, in most cases, required to repair the defect.

An important exception to the protection offered by an implied warranty happens when a retailer tells you in writing that you've bought the product "as is." In that case you often need good luck, and maybe a good lawyer, to get a faulty purchase repaired or replaced. Without a doubt, avoid buying items "as is."

Consumer protections

When it comes to full and limited warranties, the government is definitely on your side. Implied warranties are a matter of state law, and all states recognize them. What's more, federal law requires that all written guarantees be labeled "full" or "limited." It also stipulates that, for products priced at more than $15, the manufacturer or retailer allow you to read a complete description of the coverage prior to making the purchase. By law, the seller must have a copy on hand.

When you're shopping, especially for expensive appliances or other components, take advantage of the law. Ask for and carefully read all the terms of the warranty. Don't be lulled by phrases like "lifetime

guarantee" or "75-year warranty" unless the document unquestionably provides for them. If certain points are unclear (though the law says warranties must be both easy to read and easy to understand, strangely phrased boilerplate is sometimes a problem), get them cleared up before laying out your money. The key at this point is to stay cool—no matter how heated your interest in the product is—and keep from being prodded by overly zealous salespeople, who are likely to become even more so when they sense a sale at hand. In other words, don't succumb to pressure. Some retailers, believe it or not, will let you take a warranty home to read at your leisure, and for major purchases, it's not a bad idea.

If all of this sounds as though you should shop for warranties, that's not bad advice, either. Two products with similar characteristics and similar prices may or may not have similar warranties. If one provides better and longer coverage than the other, why not settle on the item with the stronger guarantee? Some buyers even bite at a slightly higher price if the product's warranty is unusually superior.

Keeping their promise

If something does go wrong, it's nice to know that a solution is only a short distance away. When you're shopping, keep your eye out for products that can be fixed at local or nearby regional service centers. Even for major purchases, some warranties require that you send the product—often at

your own expense—to a location hundreds of miles away. And once there, it may take a while to repair.

A lot of buyers think they must return the small warranty card before they're protected by the terms of the agreement. Not so, unless the company clearly states in the guarantee that it's something you have to do, a rare requirement these days. In most cases, the manufacturer includes the card, which typically contains questions about occupation, income, and the like, only as an inexpensive way to do market research.

On the other hand, in nearly every instance, you'll need a dated proof of purchase to get the ball rolling. At this point, reread the warranty, find out exactly what your rights are, and make sure you emphasize them in any correspondence with the manufacturer.

In the unlikely event that warrantied promises aren't kept, the best advice is not to dally arguing with the company. Take your complaints directly to one or more of several sources: the local office of the Federal Trade Commission; your state consumer protection agency; the Better Business Bureau; or a relevant trade association, some of which have established methods to deal with recalcitrant member firms.

WHEN THINGS JUST WEAR OUT

GETTING UP AND RUNNING AGAIN

You've found the appliance or component you're after. It's got the features you're looking for, it's the right price, and it's even got a little style. It's going to look good in your home, and for a while at least, you'll have conquered Murphy's Law (chances are, anyway).

Before you hand over the cash to your friendly retailer, however, get answers to some key questions.
• What type of warranty covers the product? What are its terms, and how long is it effective (see pages 152 and 153)?
• Is there a delivery charge if the retailer brings the appliance to your home? Is there a connecting fee? Will you have to pay for accessories or miscellaneous parts like clamps or other kinds of hardware?
• When will the equipment be delivered?
• Will the retailer disconnect and take away the old unit? If so, do you pay for the work?
• Does the retailer have a service department, or will you have to find service representatives on your own should problems develop?
• What financing plans does the retailer have? Are the terms competitive (see the box opposite)? Can you get a trade-in allowance for the old appliance?

On your own
Many buyers have new appliances or components hooked up by a pro—usually the retailer's or manufacturer's representative, who's either an employee or a member of a contract service firm—but, in any case, someone who can do the job quickly, easily, and without disrupting the household. Often, you pay for this privilege—if not directly, then indirectly in the form of a higher purchase price.

In many instances, installing a gas or electric appliance is a job a reasonably competent do-it-yourselfer can handle without much trouble. For example, if you're replacing one gas range with another, all the hard work—running a gas line to that part of the kitchen—is done. Make one hookup with a flexible gas connector, and you're cooking again.

On the other hand, if it's a completely new installation or if you're changing the position of an appliance, relying on professional help is probably the wiser course.

If you *do* decide to run gas lines yourself, check first with the local utility. Some preclude your doing this kind of work. In any event, people there will be able to fill you in on relevant aspects of the community's building code. The same goes for installing electrical circuits to supply juice for major new appliances or components. First see if you can do the work, then get an OK on your on-paper plans from an electrician.

Putting a water heater in place
Hooking up a conventional water heater isn't difficult. Even if you've decided to buy a model with larger or smaller capacity than the one you're replacing, you can usually find acceptable units in sizes identical to the old heater. If so, you won't have to work on the plumbing lines, a job that may call for experienced help.

Actually, one of the hardest parts of putting a new heater in place is getting it there. Most are located in the basement, and weigh anywhere from 125 to 200 pounds. It's a good idea to have a few extra hands around when the unit arrives. Some enterprising and

less muscular do-it-yourselfers set up a ramp in the basement, taking out the old tank and bringing in the new one through a basement window.

Usually, then, it's just a matter of reading the installation instructions and determining whether you need new plumbing or flue fittings (for gas models). Often, you won't.

Putting a washer in place
If you've ever watched an appliance service rep hook up a washer, usually in the time it takes you to write a check, you've probably thought, "That's not hard at all." And you're right, it isn't. The basics are simple: Thread hoses to valves on water supply lines— hot and cold—and insert the drain hose into a standpipe or adjacent laundry tub.

First, however, make sure the machine is level; if it's not, loads will unbalance themselves with disconcerting regularity, and the washer may even "walk" across the floor during some cycles. Check to see that all four feet are in solid contact with the floor, then tighten the locknuts securely.

Now, make the connections described above, pulling the supply hoses free of the machine and being careful not to kink them when you make the hookup. In addition, don't forget to install screens in the hose fittings.

If your machine is hooked to a standpipe, make sure the pipe is higher than the water level in the washer (to guard against overflow) and that the pipe is bigger than the hose (to prevent the washer from sucking back dirty water).

Putting a dishwasher in place
Installing a built-in dishwasher takes more carpentry skills than anything else. Most mod-

els are meant to snuggle into a 24-inch-wide space, the size of a typical base cabinet. The first step, then, is to remove an existing cabinet or design a space to fit.

Afterward, it's simply a matter of figuring out where to tie in to supply and drain lines— either at the sink, which is the simpler choice, or through the floor to basement plumbing lines.

Follow the manufacturer's instructions on materials and methods, making sure to install a shutoff valve for the supply line. Ordinarily, dishwashers drain through a hose that connects to drain work under the sink or to a garbage disposer, easy enough connections to make. In all cases, however, check local plumbing codes. Some may require different installation methods and different materials.

Putting a gas range in place
If there's a line available, your biggest job is already done. Now you need answers to certain questions. What are the proper clearances from combustible surfaces? The installation instructions should include them, and the range's rating plate definitely will. Zero clearances along the back and sides are the rule today, although most units still must be positioned at least a foot from a corner.

What connectors can you use? Flexible connectors are easier to install, but some codes prohibit them, in which case you'll have to make a "rigid" connection using a material called black steel pipe. In either instance, be sure to provide a branch-line shutoff.

Also, determine the kind of electrical connection you'll need. Some models simply plug into an ordinary household receptacle; others must be permanently joined to a wall box.

The final steps are simple: Shut off the gas, make the connections (following the manufacturer's instructions), and move in the range.

Putting a gas dryer in place

Like washers, dryers must be level to work properly. Otherwise, installing one is similar to putting in a gas range, with a single exception: You also have to provide for venting to the outside.

Vents are either rigid metal or flexible vinyl. Metal vents are slightly harder to install because they require an elbow at every change in direction. Runs of more than 10 feet usually should be made of rigid metal, with flexible vinyl reserved for short, out-in-the-open distances. Whatever the material, don't vent into a chimney or crawl space, or under a floor. Use duct tape or screws to hold joints together.

Finally, install hooded dampers on the outside to stop cold air from pounding down the vent, and think, too, about adding insulation at points along the run where the vent passes through an outside wall or unheated space.

At your service?

You got a good buy, you installed the appliance or component yourself, and it's humming along beautifully. The warranty's almost up, however, and just before it expires, you get a call from the retailer (or manufacturer or independent repair shop), who asks if you'd like to buy a service contract covering all repairs for a certain period. Good deal or not? It depends.

Many experts say that, on the average, well-made major

appliances will operate with nary a hitch for at least several years after the warranty is up and that, in most cases, it's more economical to pay for individual repairs as they're necessary than to shell out $25 to $75 a year on a service agreement you probably won't use, or use enough to justify. They say that a more reasonable strategy is to trust that all will go well during the early years (because it usually does) but to put aside a little money for repairs should you need it.

Statistically speaking, they're right. Some people, however, want a little peace of mind, no matter what the averages say. A service contract gives it to them. At the same time, families who are hard on appliances may come out ahead with a service agreement, because the charges for early repairs go up significantly.

If you *do* want a service contract, read it carefully first. Find out what's covered and what isn't, and make sure the protection doesn't begin until your warranty runs out. Ask if you can transfer the contract should you sell the appliance and if you can terminate the coverage at any time and get a refund. Large, nationally known retailers and manufacturers are generally trustworthy, but smaller companies, especially small repair shops, merit a call to the Better Business Bureau before you ink the deal.

One other thing about service contracts. Wouldn't it be a good idea to buy coverage just before Murphy's Law kicks in, and it's one thing after another? Sure. But don't count on knowing exactly when the right moment is, and don't count on fooling people who make it their business not to be fooled. The game usually goes to the other side.

FINANCING MAJOR HOUSEHOLD PURCHASES

Choosing a new washer, refrigerator, or water heater, or new heating or cooling equipment is quite different from paying for it. Major purchases can put major dents in your budget. What's the best way to get money for a big purchase when you need it?

It depends. Some families regularly squirrel away money in a liquid, interest-bearing account, which they then use as the need arises to replace expensive household necessities. When the inevitable happens, they're ready to reach into their pockets and come up with the proper sum all at once. If you can, many experts in personal finance say this is your first, best option.

Unfortunately, not everyone is able to save for every contingency. Another way to pay is to rely on the trusty piece of plastic: the revolving credit card. Doing so is both quick and initially painless, and most such financing methods allow you to tailor your payments to monthly cash flow. The biggest deterrent, especially for comparatively large amounts, is the item euphemistically called a finance

charge. It's actually an interest rate, with the interest due each month on the unpaid balance. Finance charges are often high, at least in comparison to other types of interest rates and especially if you reduce the balance slowly.

Finance companies provide another quick way to get the money, which, as with revolving credit, you can frequently repay at your own pace. On the other hand, loans of this type often carry high interest rates, as well.

So-called signature loans, arranged through a commercial bank, have become increasingly popular, particularly among remodeling-minded homeowners. Using them allows you to draw money when you need it, up to a negotiated limit, and then make regular payments at a certain interest rate, one that's typically lower than those associated with revolving credit or loans from finance companies. Usually, there's more paperwork involved, however, and you may have to wait longer for the money when you first arrange the loan.

Finally, many major retailers offer financing plans of their own for purchases over a certain figure. Check these, as well. Sometimes, you can get flexible terms, a small break on the interest rate, or both.

WHERE TO GO FOR MORE INFORMATION

Better Homes and Gardens® Books

Would you like to learn more about maintaining your house? These Better Homes and Gardens® books can help.

Better Homes and Gardens®
NEW DECORATING BOOK
How to translate ideas into workable solutions for every room in your home. Choosing a style; furniture arrangements; windows, walls, and ceilings; floors; lighting; and accessories. 433 color photos, 76 how-to illustrations, 432 pages.

Better Homes and Gardens®
DOLLAR-STRETCHING DECORATING
Save on furnishings and decorating costs without sacrificing style or comfort. Filled with easy-to-carry-out ideas, practical suggestions, do-it-yourself projects, and how-to drawings. 160 color photos, 125 illustrations, 192 pages.

Better Homes and Gardens®
COMPLETE GUIDE TO HOME REPAIR, MAINTENANCE, AND IMPROVEMENT
Inside your home, outside your home, your home's systems, basics you should know. Anatomy and step-by-step drawings illustrate components, tools, techniques, and finishes. 515 how-to techniques; 75 charts; 2,734 illustrations; 552 pages.

Better Homes and Gardens®
COMPLETE GUIDE TO GARDENING
A comprehensive guide for beginners and experienced gardeners. Houseplants, lawns and landscaping, trees and shrubs, greenhouses, insects and diseases. 461 color photos, 434 how-to illustrations, 37 charts, 552 pages.

Better Homes and Gardens®
STEP-BY-STEP BUILDING SERIES
A series of do-it-yourself building books that provides step-by-step illustrations and how-to information for starting and finishing many common construction projects and repair jobs around your house. More than 90 projects and 1,200 illustrations in this series of six 96-page books:
STEP-BY-STEP BASIC PLUMBING
STEP-BY-STEP BASIC WIRING
STEP-BY-STEP BASIC CARPENTRY
STEP-BY-STEP HOUSEHOLD REPAIRS
STEP-BY-STEP MASONRY & CONCRETE
STEP-BY-STEP CABINETS & SHELVES

Other Sources of Information

Many manufacturers and professional associations offer information that can help you maintain your home.

American Gas Association
1515 Wilson Blvd.
Arlington, VA 22209

American Hardboard
Association
887-B Wilmette Rd.
Palatine, IL 60067

American Home Lighting
Institute
230 N. Michigan Ave.
Chicago, IL 60601

American Olean Tile Company
Public Relations Department
1000 Cannon Ave.
Lansdale, PA 19446

American Plywood Association
P.O. Box 11700
Tacoma, WA 98411

American Society of Interior
Designers
730 Fifth Ave.
New York, NY 10019

Armstrong World Industries
(resilient flooring)
Consumer Services
P.O. Box 3001
Lancaster, PA 17604

Asphalt Roofing Manufacturers
Association
6288 Montrose Rd.
Rockville, MD 20852

Association of Home
Appliance Manufacturers
20 N. Wacker Dr.
Chicago, IL 60606

Bruce Hardwood Floors
Marketing Department
P.O. Box 220100
Dallas, TX 75222

California Redwood
Association, Suite 3100
591 Redwood Highway,
Mill Valley, CA 94941

Carpet Cushion Council
P.O. Box 465
Southfield, MO 48037

Carpet & Rug Institute
P.O. Box 2048
Dalton, GA 30720

Ceilings and Interior Systems
Contractors Association
1800 Pickwick Ave.
Glenview, IL 60025

Cellulose Manufacturers
Association
5908 Columbia Pike
Baileys Crossroads, VA 22041

Congoleum Corporation
Resilient Flooring Division
195 Belgrove Dr.
Kearny, NJ 07032

Exterior Insulation
Manufacturers Association
1000 Vermont Ave., NW
Suite 1200
Washington, DC 20005

Federal Trade Commission
Bureau of Consumer
Protection
Washington, DC 20580

Furniture Industry Consumer
Advisory Panel
P.O. Box 951
High Point, NC 27261

Gypsum Association
1603 Orrington Ave.
Evanston, IL 60201

Major Appliance Consumer
Action Panel
20 N. Wacker Dr.
Chicago, IL 60606

Man-Made Fiber Producers
Association, Suite 310
1150 17th St., NW
Washington, DC 20036

National Association for
Bedding Manufacturers
1235 Jefferson Davis Highway
Arlington, VA 22202

National Association of
Furniture Manufacturers
8401 Connecticut Ave.
Suite 911
Washington, DC 20015

National Association of the
Remodeling Industry
11 E. 44th St.
New York, NY 10017

ACKNOWLEDGMENTS

National Center for a
Barrier-Free Environment
Suite 1006
1140 Connecticut Ave., NW
Washington, DC 20036

National Housewares
Manufacturers Association
1130 Merchandise Mart
Chicago, IL 60654

National Kitchen and Bath
Association
114 Main St.
Hackettstown, NJ 07840

Red Cedar Shingle & Handsplit
Shake Bureau, Suite 275
515-116th Ave., NE
Bellevue, WA 98004

St. Regis Forest Products
1019 Pacific Ave.
Tacoma, WA 98401

Tile Council of America
Box 326
Princeton, NJ 08540

U.S. Plywood
Division of Champion
International
777 Third Ave.
New York, NY 10017

Vermont Marble Company
61 Main St.
Proctor, VT 05765

Vinyl siding information:
Bird Incorporated
Withrow Lane
Bardstown, KY 40004

Western Wood Products
Association
1500 Yeon Building
Portland, OR 97204

The Wool Bureau, Inc.
360 Lexington Ave.
New York, NY 10017

Consumer Hotline Numbers
Many manufacturers,
associations, and consumer
groups list toll free telephone

numbers that you can call for
assistance or information.

Admiral Home Appliances
Bloomington, IL
US, except AK, HI, IL:
800/447-8371
IL: 800/322-6302

Armstrong World Industries
Lancaster, PA
US, except AK, HI, PA:
800/233-3823
PA: 800/732-0048

Broan Mfg. Co.
Hartford, WI
US, except AK, HI, WI:
800/558-1711

Emerson Electric
Bennettsville, SC
Continental US, PR, VI,
except SC: 800/845-9001

General Electric Answer
Center/Consumer Product
Information
Louisville, KY
Continental US, PR, VI:
800/626-2000

Jacuzzi Whirlpool Bath
Walnut Creek, CA
Continental US, PR, VI,
except CA: 800/227-0710

Litton Microwave Cooking
Minneapolis, MN
Continental US, PR, VI,
except MN: 800/328-3338

Major Appliance Consumer
Action Panel
Chicago, IL
US, except AK, HI, IL:
800/621-0477

Montgomery Ward, Inc.
Oklahoma City, OK
US, except AK, HI, OK:
800/522-8388

Nusash Windows
Tridelphia, WV
DC, DE, IN, KY, MD, NC, NJ,
NY, OH, PA, SC, TN, VA:
800/624-5406

Reliance Water Heaters
Ashland City, TN
Continental US, PR, VI,
except TN: 800/251-4054

Ridge Overhead Garage Doors
Monmouth, NJ
US, except AK, HI, NY:
800/631-5656
NJ: 800 872-4982

Rug Doctor Inc.
Fenton, MO
US, except AK, HI, MO:
800/821-3161

Sub-Zero Freezer Corp.
Madison, WI
Continental US, PR, VI,
except WI: 800/356-5826

Thermasol
Leonia, NJ
Continental US, PR, VI,
except NJ: 800/631-1601

Thomasville Furniture
Thomasville, NC
US, except AK, HI, NC:
800/225-0265
NC: 800/672-4224

Whirlpool Corporation Cool
Line Service
Benton Harbor, MI
US, except AK, HI, MI:
800/253-1301
AK, HI: 800/253-1121
MI: 800/632-2243

**Interior Designers
And Architects**
The following is a page-by-
page listing of the interior
designers, architects, and
project designers whose work
appears in this book.

Pages 12-13
  Dan Nexovic, CKD;
  Betsey Johnson
Pages 16-17
  Barbara and Tommy Bryan
Pages 18-19
  Dee and Stephen Arnold
Pages 22-23
  Decks by Notch and
  Steve Brena
Pages 34-35
  Rod Garrett
Pages 80-81
  Louise Rosenfeld,
  ASID/Arrangements
Pages 92-93
  Barry Berkus
Pages 104-105
  Robert Turner
Pages 132-133
  Thomas J. Eldridge, Jr.

**Photographers
and Illustrators**
We extend our thanks to the
following photographers and
illustrators, whose creative
talents and technical skills
contributed much to this book.

Ernest Braun
Hedrich-Blessing
Hopkins Associates
Scott Little
Maris/Semel
John Rogers

**Associations
and Companies**
Our appreciation goes to the
following associations and
companies for providing
information and materials for
this book.

Chim Chim Cheree Chimney
  Sweeps
Clive Small Engine Repair
Des Moines Seed and Nursery
Domestic Aide
Duncan Sanitary Products
Lumberman's Wholesale Co.
Pella Rolscreen Co.
Rowat Cut Stone Co.
True Value Hardware

INDEX